Cycle
Tours

In & around the Lake District National Park, the Lune Valley & the Eden Valley

Nick Cotton

Publisher: Cycle Tours is a joint venture between CycleCity Guides and Cordee

CycleCity Guides
The Welsh Mill
Parkhill Drive
Frome
BA11 2LE
T: +44 (0)1373 453533

info@cyclecityguides.co.uk
www.cyclecityguides.co.uk

Cordee
11 Jacknell Road
Dodwells Bridge Industrial Estate
Hinckley
LE10 3BS
T: +44 (0)1455 611 185

charlie@cordee.co.uk
www.cordee.co.uk

ISBN: 978-1 904207603

Printed by: Victoria Litho
Picture credits: Nick Cotton

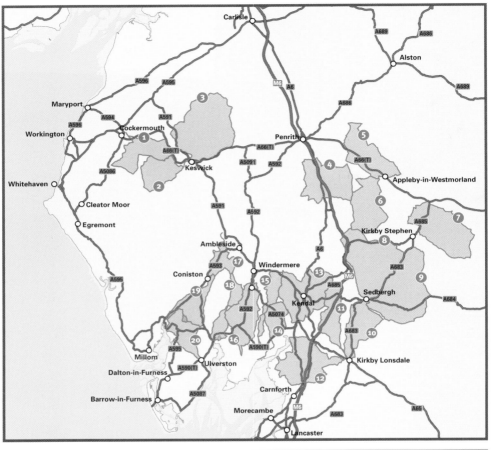

Quick reference chart

Grades

▲	Easy	
▲▲	Easy / Moderate	The grade is based on the amount of climbing
▲▲▲	Moderate	involved rather than the distance covered.
▲▲▲▲	Moderate / Strenuous	
▲▲▲▲▲	Strenuous	

In & around the Lake District National Park, the Lune Valley & the Eden Valley

The Lake District National Park, the Eden Valley and the Lune Valley boast some of the most stunning mountain scenery in the country, providing a dramatic backdrop to almost all of the rides featured here. More than 15 million visits are made to the area each year; this is clearly a double-edged sword - lots of visitors means lots of tourist services such as pubs, cafés, bike shops and accommodation but as the vast majority arrive by car, this also can mean lots of extra traffic.

The rides have been designed to use quieter roads. In the case of beautiful roads which are also busy roads, they are very rarely included in the rides: safety concerns are paramount. For those of you who have the flexibility to choose, there will always be times of the day, week and year when, with the exception of perhaps half a dozen busy A roads, you can ride safely almost anywhere in Cumbria without seeing much traffic. Weekdays are quieter than weekends; avoid school holidays, half terms and Bank Holidays if you can; and if you are prepared to get up really early in midsummer, it is light from 4 o'clock in the morning! Mid April to mid June or mid September to the end of October are quieter times when the days are long enough to have a full day out.

The rides are divided into three main areas: the first is around Cockermouth and Keswick where three rides explore the stunning landscape either side of Bassenthwaite Lake. To the west lie Wythop Woods, Whinlatter Forest, Loweswater, Crummock Water and Buttermere; to the east of Bassenthwaite is the classic circuit around the back of Skiddaw to Caldbeck.

The second area covers the southeast of Cumbria, encompassing the upper Eden Valley and the Lune Valley, with rides starting from the handsome towns of Appleby, Kirkby Stephen, Sedbergh and Kirkby Lonsdale. The weather tends to be drier here as the two valleys lie in the rain shadow of the Lakeland Fells. These rides also offer views of the Pennines, rising to 2930ft (893m) on Cross Fell and of the Howgills, the great 'sleeping elephants' lying to the north of Sedbergh. This area tends to be quieter than the Lake District.

The final area features rides in and around the southern half of the Lake District National Park, largely within a boundary formed by Grasmere, Kendal, Grange over Sands and Broughton in Furness. There are dramatic views of many of the central lakes and fells including those to be enjoyed from the Windermere Ferry, featured on the ride north from Backbarrow. You may well be pleasantly surprised that there are so many quiet lanes to explore in such a popular tourist area. Choose your time well and you will enjoy your rides even more!

Other useful information

Easy, traffic-free cycling for families and novices

Although the rides in this book are aimed at reasonably fit cyclists who are happy riding on roads, there may be times when your preference is for a ride that is also suitable for children or 'novice' cyclists. Listed below are some of the easier, flatter, traffic-free routes in the area.

Canals, seaside and lakes

1. Northwest shore of Windermere

From the western terminus of the Windermere ferry (on the Far Sawrey side) north along the shore of Windermere there is a 4-mile ride to the church at Low Wray on a mixture of tarmac and wide stone track. Go to **www.lakedistrict.gov.uk** and click on **'Visiting - things to do'**

2. Lancaster Canal

(Just outside Cumbria). The towpath of the Lancaster Canal from Carnforth south to Lancaster (10 miles) is of a good standard and passable on most types of bike. Go to **www. celebratingcycling.org**

3. Morecambe Bay

(Just outside Cumbria). There is a fine 5-mile ride along the promenade from near Heysham north past Morecambe towards Hest Bank. Go to **www. celebratingcycling.org**

Railway paths

1. Keswick to Threlkeld

A 3-mile railway path runs east from Kendal Leisure Pool to Threlkeld. Go to **www.lakedistrict. gov.uk** and click on **'Visiting - things to do'**

2. Workington - Whitehaven - Rowrah

There is a high density of railway paths on the west coast of Cumbria. This traffic-free trail starts at Camerton, between Cockermouth and Workington, runs through Workington and Distington to Whitehaven then turns inland through Cleator Moor to Rowrah. Go to **www. lakedistrict.gov.uk** and click on **'Visiting - things to do'**

3. Lancaster & Morecambe railway paths

(Just outside Cumbria). A railway path starts at Caton, about 5 miles northwest of Lancaster on the A683, passes through Lancaster and reaches the coast at Glasson Dock. A spur leads from the Millennium Bridge in the centre of Lancaster to Morecambe. Go to **www.celebratingcycling.org**

Woodland

1. Grizedale

Several waymarked routes aimed at families although none are flat. Go to **www.forestry.gov.uk** and search **'Grizedale Cycling'**.

2. Whinlatter

You can cycle where you like but Whinlatter is even hillier than Grizedale! Go to **www.forestry. gov.uk** and search **'Whinlatter Cycling'**.

Sustrans and the National Cycle Network

Go to **www.sustrans.org.uk** click on **'Sustrans near you'** then **'North of England'** then **'Cumbria'**. There are downloads, details of free leaflets and details of NCN routes in the region.

Cycle shops in the area

See
www.icumbria.co.uk/local/cycle-shops/
www.iyorkshire.co.uk/local/cycle-shops/
www.ilancashire.co.uk/local/cycle-shops/
www.thecyclepeople.com

Legend to 1:50,000 maps

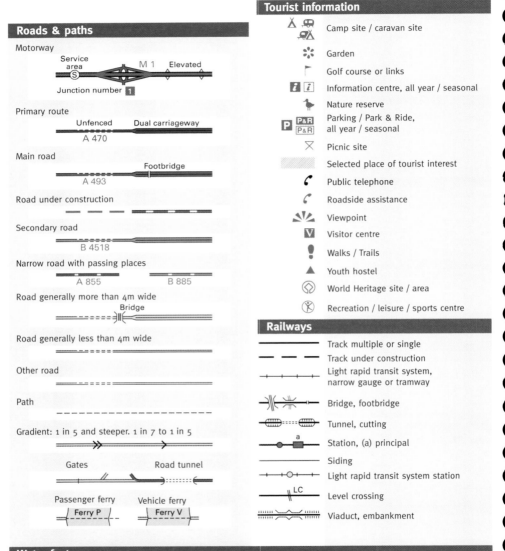

Roads & paths

Motorway

Service area (S)   M 1   Elevated

Junction number **1**

Primary route

Unfenced   Dual carriageway

A 470

Main road

Footbridge

A 493

Road under construction

Secondary road

B 4518

Narrow road with passing places

A 855   B 885

Road generally more than 4m wide

Bridge

Road generally less than 4m wide

Other road

Path

Gradient: 1 in 5 and steeper. 1 in 7 to 1 in 5

Gates   Road tunnel

Passenger ferry   Vehicle ferry

Ferry P   Ferry V

Tourist information

Camp site / caravan site
Garden
Golf course or links
i **i**	Information centre, all year / seasonal
Nature reserve
P **P&R** **P&R**	Parking / Park & Ride, all year / seasonal
✕	Picnic site
Selected place of tourist interest
Public telephone
Roadside assistance
Viewpoint
V	Visitor centre
Walks / Trails
▲	Youth hostel
World Heritage site / area
Recreation / leisure / sports centre

Railways

Track multiple or single
Track under construction
Light rapid transit system, narrow gauge or tramway
Bridge, footbridge
Tunnel, cutting
Station, (a) principal
Siding
Light rapid transit system station
Level crossing
Viaduct, embankment

Water features

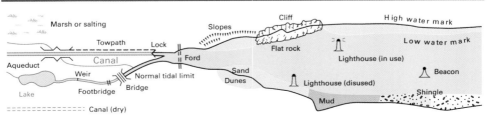

4

General features

 Cutting, embankment

 Landfill site

 Coniferous wood

 Non-coniferous wood

 Mixed wood

 Orchard

 Park or ornamental ground

 Forestry Commission land

 National Trust - always open

 National Trust - limited access, observe local signs

National Trust for Scotland - always open

National Trust for Scotland - limited access, observe local signs

 Electricity transmission line (pylons shown at standard spacing)

> --> --> Pipe line (arrow indicates direction of flow)

 Building

 Important building (selected)

 Bus or coach station

 Glass structure

Ⓗ Hospital

 Place of worship with tower

 Place of worship with spire, dome or minaret

+ Place of worship

 Mast

Ï Ï Wind pump / wind turbine

 Windmill with or without sails

+ Graticule intersection at 5' intervals

Rock features

Outcrop Cliff Scree

Public rights of way
(not applicable in Scotland)

---------------- Footpath
-·---·---·--- Restricted byway
------------ Bridleway
-+-+-+-+-+- Byway open to all traffic

Public rights of way shown have been taken from local authority definitive maps and later amendments. The symbols show the defined route so far as the scale of mapping will allow.

The representation on this map of any other road, track or path is no evidence of the existence of a right of way.

Other public access

· · · · Other route with public access

◆ ◆ ◆ National Trail, European Long Distance Path, Long Distance Route, selected Recreational Routes

● ● ● On-road cycle route

○ ○ ○ Off-road cycle route

4 National Cycle Network Number

8 Regional Cycle Network Number

Danger Area Firing and test ranges in the area Danger! Observe warning notices

Boundaries

+ — + — + National
+ — + — + District
— · — · — · — County, region or island area

National Park

Abbreviations

CH	Clubhouse
PH	Public house
PC	Public convenience (in rural area)
TH	Town Hall, Guildhall or equivalent
CG	Cattle grid
P	Post office
MP	Milepost
MS	Mile stone

Antiquities

+ Position of antiquity that cannot be drawn to scale

☆ ···· Visible earthwork

VILLA Roman

Castle Non-Roman

⚔ Battlefield (with date)

Heights

═50═ Contours are at 10 metre vertical intervals

·144 Heights are to the nearest metre above mean sea level

Heights shown close to a triangulation pillar refer to the station height at ground level and not necessarily to the summit

Abbreviations and instructions

Instructions are given concisely to make them easy to follow while out riding. Remember to read one or two instructions ahead so that you do not miss a turning. This is most likely when you have to turn off a road / track you have been following for a while and are marked **Easy to miss** to warn you.

If there appears to be a contradiction between the instructions and what you actually see, always refer to the map. There are many reasons why, over the course of time, instructions may be subject to change with new roads, new junctions and new signposts.

Directions (all directions are given in bold)

L	left
R	right
SA	straight ahead
bear **L** or **R**	a turn which is less than 90 degrees (right-angle) at a fork in the road or on a sharp bend so that your course appears to be straight ahead; this is often written as 'in effect **SA**'
sharp **L** or **R**	a turn more acute than a right-angle
L or **R** sharply back on yourself	almost a U-turn
R then **L**	normally a T-junction where the next turn is visible from the first
R then first **L**	the second turning may be some distance from the first, ie '**R** then after ½ mile first **L**'

Junctions

T-j	T-junction, a junction where you have to give way
X-roads	crossroads, a junction where you may or may not have to give way
offset X-roads	the four roads are not in the form of a perfect cross and you will have to turn left then right, or vice versa, to continue the route

Signs

'Placename 2'	the words in quotation marks are those that appear on the signs, the numbers indicate the distance in miles unless stated otherwise
(NS)	not signposted

Instructions

An example of an easy instruction is:

4 At T-j at end of Smith Road by the White Swan Inn turn **R** on Brown Street 'Greentown 2, Redville 3'

There is more information in this instruction than you would normally need but things do change: pubs may close down and signs may be replaced, removed or vandalised.

An example of a difficult instruction is:

8 Easy to miss: shortly after the brow of the hill, on fast descent, first **R** (NS)

As you can see, there is no T-junction or 'Give Way' sign to halt you in your tracks, no signpost indicating where the right turn will take you and in addition you are picking up speed on a downhill, so you need to have your wits about you not to miss the turning.

Overview pages

Start
This is the suggested start point, coinciding with Instruction 1 on the map. There is no reason why you should not start at another point if it is more convenient.

Busy roads
These rides aim to keep to an absolute minimum time spent on busy roads but there are sometimes unavoidable sections where lane networks do not neatly link together. These busy roads are mentioned so that you are mentally prepared to deal with traffic, especially if there are children or less experienced cyclists in the group.

Terrain
This brief description of the terrain covered by the route should be read in conjunction with the cross-profile diagram at the foot of the page to help you plan your journey.

Refreshments
More than three pubs or a mixture of pubs, cafés and tearooms in any one place is indicated by 'Lots of choice'. Otherwise, names of pubs, cafés and tearooms are listed, where possible with telephone numbers so that you can call ahead to check on opening times and when food is served.

Distance
The distance (shown in miles and kilometres) is, of course, that from the beginning to the end of the ride. However, if you wish to shorten the ride because of tiredness, mechanical problems, a change in the weather or simply lack of time then the maps enable you to do so.

Grade
There are five grades of difficulty:
Easy
Easy / Moderate
Moderate
Moderate / Strenuous
Strenuous
The grade is based on the amount of climbing involved rather than the distance covered.

Ride 3

Overview
On-road ● 33 miles / 53 kilometres ● Moderate

Start
Keswick Leisure Pool, on Brundholme Road, signposted off the A5271 on the north side of Keswick (near the A66 roundabout)

Parking
As above

Busy roads
About 2 miles on the A591 to the west of Keswick, near the end of the ride ⓫ to ⓰

Terrain
Gentle gradients on first half of ride. Hillier with longer climbs on second half. Longest climb - 425ft (130m) west of Caldbeck

Nearest railway
Penrith or Wigton

Refreshments
Keswick
Lots of choice

Threlkeld
Horse & Farrier PH
T: 017687 79688
Salutation Inn
T: 017687 79614

Mungrisdale
Mill Inn
T: 017687 79632

Hesket Newmarket
Old Crown PH
T: 016974 78288
Tearoom
T: 016974 78229

Caldbeck
Watermill Café
T: 016974 78267
Oddfellows Arms PH
T: 016974 78227
Old Smithy Tearoom
T: 016974 78246

Bassenthwaite
Sun Inn
T: 017687 76439

Other rides nearby

Ride 3

Ride 2
Page 14

Map pages
Route overviews show how the maps have been laid out on the pages. Page numbers are shown in the corners. The diagrams show start points, route direction and some of the villages on or near the route.

Other rides nearby
Schematic map showing where nearby rides overlap. Shorter or longer rides can be created by mixing and matching rides.

Cross-profile
Shows heights in metres and distance travelled. Places along the route are shown.

7

Cockermouth, Lorton Vale & Whinlatter

This spectacular ride south from Cockermouth explores the northwest corner of the Lake District National Park visiting the delights of Loweswater, Lorton Vale, Whinlatter and Wythop Woods. There is a Wordsworth connection at two points along the ride: the poet was born in a Georgian house at the end of Cockermouth's main street and wrote a poem ('Yew Trees') about High Lorton: *'There is a yew tree, pride of Lorton Vale / Which to this day stands single, in the midst / Of its own darkness, as it stood of yore'*. The ride climbs

southeast from Cockermouth to Roundclose Hill before dropping to cross the River Cocker and heading south to the beauty of Loweswater, dominated by the dramatic outline of Mellbreak. The section up Lorton Vale offers fine views east towards Grasmoor and Hopegill Head. Recross the Cocker and climb steeply up to Whinlatter on

a mix of tarmac and a wide stone forest track that avoids the B5292, a road which can get busy. There is a very good café at Whinlatter Visitor Centre. A long, wooded, off-road descent follows, dropping down to the old road through Thornthwaite, now bypassed by the A66. A second, shorter but much steeper and rougher off-road section climbs through Wythop Woods to reach what feels like the hidden, forgotten valley of Wythop Beck. Quiet lanes lead back towards Cockermouth.

NB Although the off-road sections are all on the National Cycle Network, short stretches are quite steep and rough, especially through Wythop Woods. The ride can be done on road bikes (with short sections where you will have to push) but you should fit 28mm or 32mm tyres.

Overview
30 miles / 48 kilometres ● Strenuous

Start
Cockermouth Tourist Information Centre / Town Hall off Market Place

Parking
Bitterbeck car park near to the Tourist Information Centre (off Market Place)

Busy roads
● The B5292 Lorton Road at the start of the ride ❸

● The road alongside Loweswater can get busy in high season ❽ to ❾

● Short section on B5292 near to Whinlatter Pass ⓬

Terrain
First half of the ride is fairly easy with one short steep climb after Mosser. Two big climbs: the first from Low Lorton to Whinlatter Pass (800ft / 245m) and the second from Bassenthwaite Lake up through Wythop Woods (525ft / 160m)

Nearest railway
Workington

Refreshments
Cockermouth
Lots of choice

Loweswater
Kirkstile Inn
T: 01900 85219

Low Lorton
Wheatsheaf Inn
T: 01900 85199

Whinlatter Visitor Centre
Siskins Café
T: 017687 74410

Other rides nearby

Ride 1

Ride 2
Page 14

Map pages

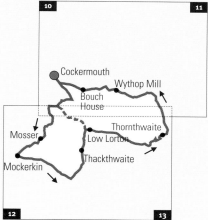

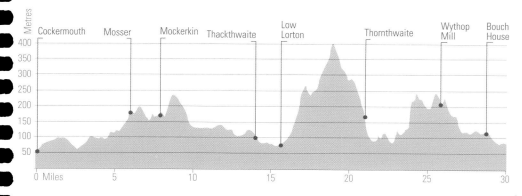

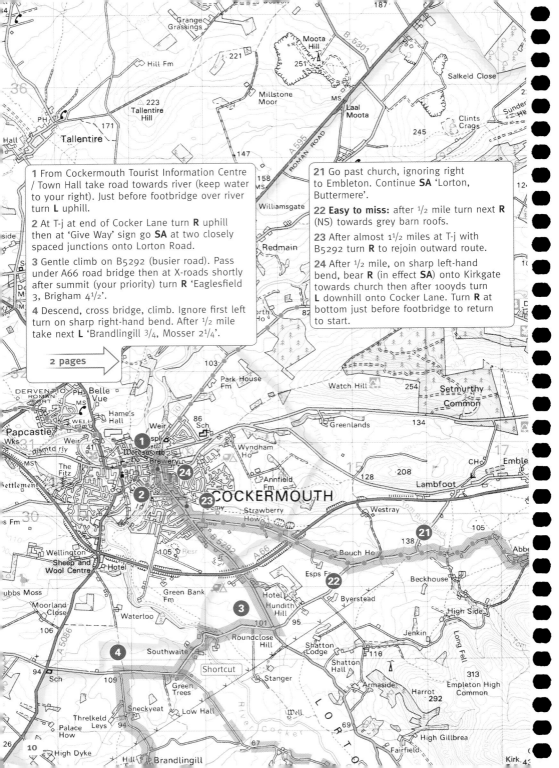

1 From Cockermouth Tourist Information Centre / Town Hall take road towards river (keep water to your right). Just before footbridge over river turn **L** uphill.

2 At T-j at end of Cocker Lane turn **R** uphill then at 'Give Way' sign go **SA** at two closely spaced junctions onto Lorton Road.

3 Gentle climb on B5292 (busier road). Pass under A66 road bridge then at X-roads shortly after summit (your priority) turn **R** 'Eaglesfield 3, Brigham 4½'.

4 Descend, cross bridge, climb. Ignore first left turn on sharp right-hand bend. After ½ mile take next **L** 'Brandlingill ¾, Mosser 2¼'.

2 pages →

21 Go past church, ignoring right to Embleton. Continue **SA** 'Lorton, Buttermere'.

22 Easy to miss: after ½ mile turn next **R** (NS) towards grey barn roofs.

23 After almost 1½ miles at T-j with B5292 turn **R** to rejoin outward route.

24 After ½ mile, on sharp left-hand bend, bear **R** (in effect **SA**) onto Kirkgate towards church then after 100yds turn **L** downhill onto Cocker Lane. Turn **R** at bottom just before footbridge to return to start.

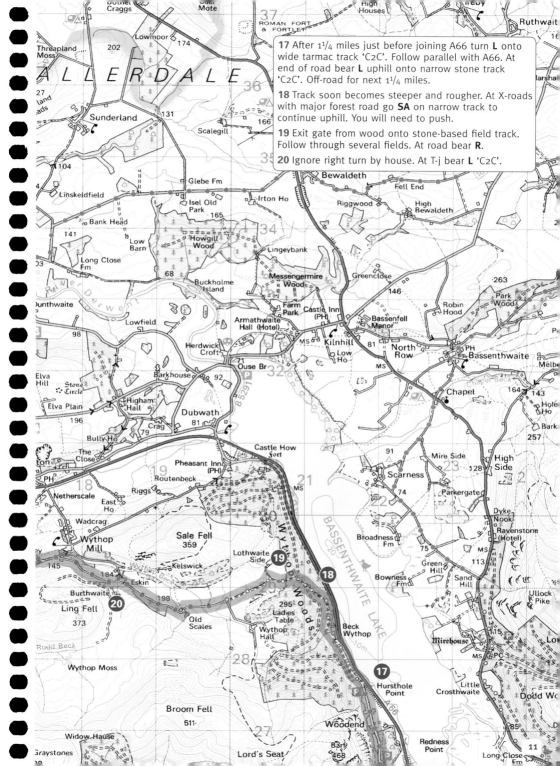

17 After 1¼ miles just before joining A66 turn **L** onto wide tarmac track 'C2C'. Follow parallel with A66. At end of road bear **L** uphill onto narrow stone track 'C2C'. Off-road for next 1¼ miles.

18 Track soon becomes steeper and rougher. At X-roads with major forest road go **SA** on narrow track to continue uphill. You will need to push.

19 Exit gate from wood onto stone-based field track. Follow through several fields. At road bear **R**.

20 Ignore right turn by house. At T-j bear **L** 'C2C'.

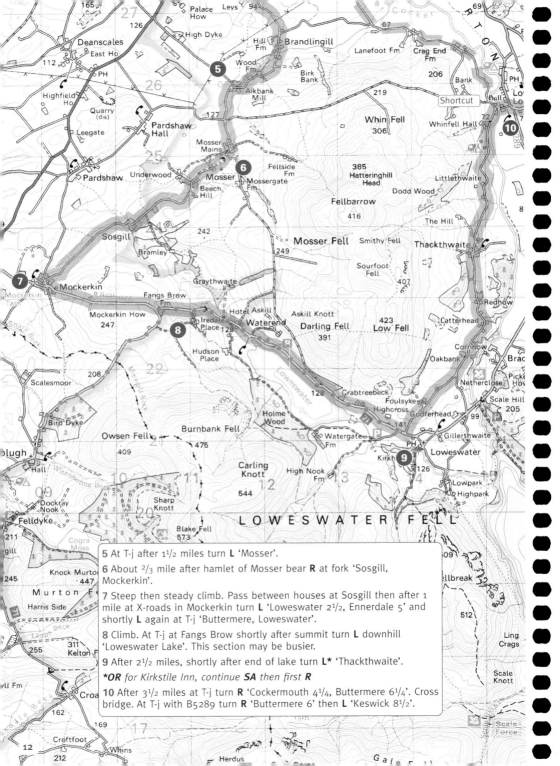

5 At T-j after 1½ miles turn **L** 'Mosser'.

6 About ⅔ mile after hamlet of Mosser bear **R** at fork 'Sosgill, Mockerkin'.

7 Steep then steady climb. Pass between houses at Sosgill then after 1 mile at X-roads in Mockerkin turn **L** 'Loweswater 2½, Ennerdale 5' and shortly **L** again at T-j 'Buttermere, Loweswater'.

8 Climb. At T-j at Fangs Brow shortly after summit turn **L** downhill 'Loweswater Lake'. This section may be busier.

9 After 2½ miles, shortly after end of lake turn **L*** 'Thackthwaite'.

*OR for Kirkstile Inn, continue **SA** then first **R***

10 After 3½ miles at T-j turn **R** 'Cockermouth 4¼, Buttermere 6¼'. Cross bridge. At T-j with B5289 turn **R** 'Buttermere 6' then **L** 'Keswick 8½'.

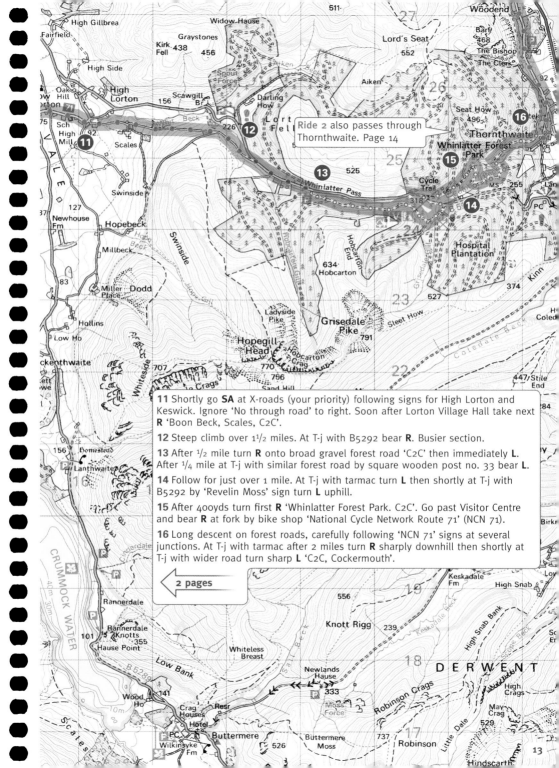

Ride 2 also passes through Thornthwaite. Page 14

11 Shortly go **SA** at X-roads (your priority) following signs for High Lorton and Keswick. Ignore 'No through road' to right. Soon after Lorton Village Hall take next **R** 'Boon Beck, Scales, C2C'.

12 Steep climb over 1½ miles. At T-j with B5292 bear **R**. Busier section.

13 After ½ mile turn **R** onto broad gravel forest road 'C2C' then immediately **L**. After ¼ mile at T-j with similar forest road by square wooden post no. 33 bear **L**.

14 Follow for just over 1 mile. At T-j with tarmac turn **L** then shortly at T-j with B5292 by 'Revelin Moss' sign turn **L** uphill.

15 After 400yds turn first **R** 'Whinlatter Forest Park. C2C'. Go past Visitor Centre and bear **R** at fork by bike shop 'National Cycle Network Route 71' (NCN 71).

16 Long descent on forest roads, carefully following 'NCN 71' signs at several junctions. At T-j with tarmac after 2 miles turn **R** sharply downhill then shortly at T-j with wider road turn sharp **L** 'C2C, Cockermouth'.

2 pages

13

Keswick, Crummock Water & Newlands Pass

This ride explores the area to the southwest of Keswick, neatly avoiding the busy A66 via a series of dead-end roads, a footbridge over the River Derwent and wooded lanes between Portinscale and Thornthwaite. The climb up to Whinlatter Visitor Centre uses a wide stone forest track that forms part of National Cycle Network Route 71 (part of the famous C2C Cycle Route). If you are on a lightweight road bike and are not concerned about traffic you may prefer to stay on road, using the B5292 to climb to the top of the hill.

Whichever option you choose, a coffee stop at Siskins Café in Whinlatter Visitor Centre is highly recommended, this being the only opportunity for refreshments between Braithwaite and Buttermere. A long descent follows with superb views across Lorton Vale to Mosser Fell and Loweswater Fell. At the bottom of the hill you join the B5289 for almost 5 miles, a stunning road alongside Crummock Water, but one which is best enjoyed midweek outside school holidays as it can get busy, especially on fine summer weekends. The village of

Buttermere has a pub and a tearoom: refreshments may well be in order as you are faced with one of the toughest climbs in the book - six black arrows in less than a mile at the top of the 750ft (230m) climb to Newlands Hause. This is one of the hills on the famous Fred Whitton Challenge: a 112-mile ride climbing the six highest passes in the Lake District (the others are Kirkstone, Honister, Whinlatter, Hard Knott and Wrynose). Once at the top of Newlands Hause you are faced with a wonderful long descent down the valley back to Keswick, rejoining the outward route just south of Portinscale.

NB The route described uses a wide stone forest track to climb through Whinlatter Forest up to the Visitor Centre to avoid the B5292. Road bikes are fine although it is better to fit 28mm or 32mm tyres. Alternatively, just use the B5292, although this can get busy. The ride is best done midweek, outside school holidays: try early May to mid June or mid September to the end of October.

Overview
26 miles / 42 kilometres ● Strenuous

Start
Keswick Leisure Pool, on Brundholme Road, signposted off the A5271 on the north side of Keswick (near the A66 roundabout)

Parking
As above

Busy roads
The ride is best done midweek outside school holidays

● The B5292 west of Whinlatter Visitor Centre (gently downhill) **11** to **12**

● The B5289 past Crummock Water can get busy **14** to **15**

Terrain
Hilly with two tough climbs: the first from Braithwaite off-road through woodland to Whinlatter Visitor Centre (790ft / 240m), the second from Crummock Water to the top of Newlands Hause (750ft / 230m)

Nearest railway
None nearby - the nearest are in Workington or Penrith

Refreshments
Keswick
Lots of choice

Whinlatter Visitor Centre
Siskins Café
T: 017687 74410

Buttermere
Bridge Hotel
T: 017687 70252
Syke Farm Tearoom
T: 017687 70277

Swinside
Swinside Inn
T: 017687 78253

Other rides nearby

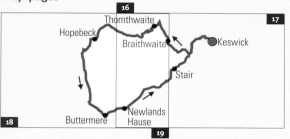

Ride 1
Page 8

Ride 2

Ride 3
Page 20

Map pages

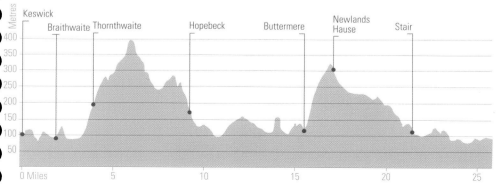

Ride 1 also passes through Thornthwaite. Page 8

3 Cross footbridge. At T-j after Derwentwater Hotel turn **L** 'Grange 4, Newlands Valley'.

4 At fork after ²/3 mile bear **R** 'Ullock 1'.

5 At T-j turn **R** 'Braithwaite ³/4'. Cross bridge then at T-j turn **R** 'Braithwaite ¹/2'.

6 Follow road over second bridge and signs for 'Whinlatter Pass and Lorton'. At X-roads by Royal Oak PH go **SA** uphill 'C2C, NCN 71'.

7 After ³/4 mile at T-j bear **L** (NS).

8 Easy to miss: go through Thornthwaite ignoring several left turns. About 100yds before 'End of Speed Limit' signs, opposite house on right called 'The Hollins', bear **L** uphill by 3-way National Cycle Network signpost 'C2C Whitehaven'. Shortly turn sharp **L** uphill on broad stone forest track.

9 Climb steeply on forest road for 1¹/4 miles. At T-j by wooden post no. 12 turn **R** 'NCN 71'.

10 After ¹/2 mile at T-j turn sharp **L** uphill 'NCN 71' then shortly at next T-j bear **L** past Post no. 14 (same sign).

11 Go past Whinlatter Visitor Centre following 'Exit' signs. At T-j with B5292 turn **R**. Busier section but gently downhill.

3 pages →

16 Climb steeply for 1¹/4 miles. After long descent, ignore first right to Newlands Church. Take next **R** 'Stair ¹/4, Portinscale 2¹/2, Grange 4'.

17 Go past Swinside Inn and follow signs for Portinscale. At T-j bear **L** 'Portinscale 1¹/2, Keswick 3'.

18 Rejoin outward route. Shortly after passing Portinscale Tearoom on left, turn **R** on left-hand bend onto no through road to go past Derwentwater Hotel.

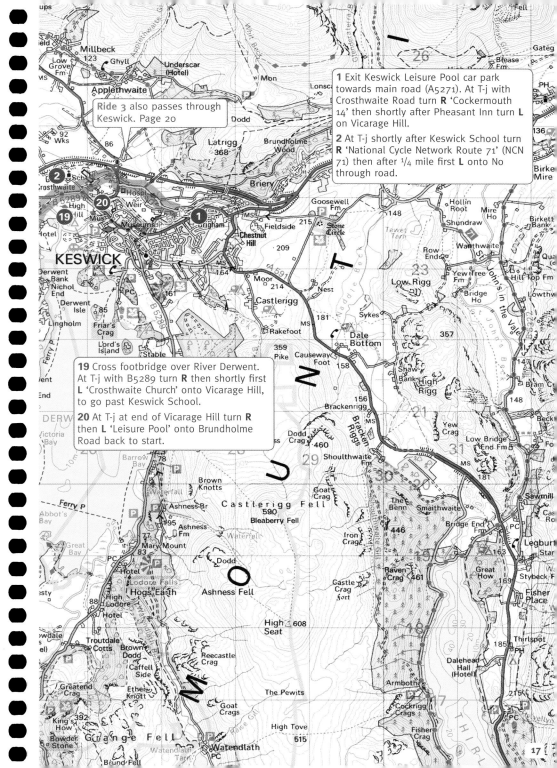

1 Exit Keswick Leisure Pool car park towards main road (A5271). At T-j with Crosthwaite Road turn **R** 'Cockermouth 14' then shortly after Pheasant Inn turn **L** on Vicarage Hill.

2 At T-j shortly after Keswick School turn **R** 'National Cycle Network Route 71' (NCN 71) then after 1/4 mile first **L** onto No through road.

Ride 3 also passes through Keswick. Page 20

19 Cross footbridge over River Derwent. At T-j with B5289 turn **R** then shortly first **L** 'Crosthwaite Church' onto Vicarage Hill, to go past Keswick School.

20 At T-j at end of Vicarage Hill turn **R** then **L** 'Leisure Pool' onto Brundholme Road back to start.

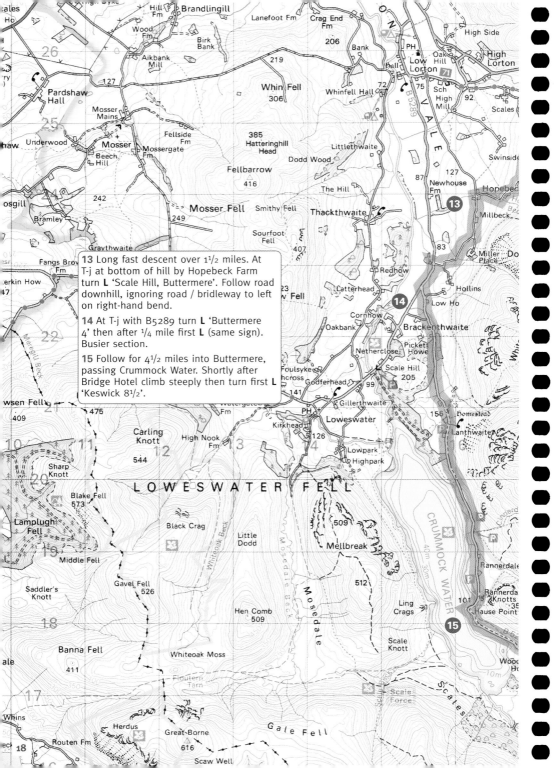

13 Long fast descent over 1½ miles. At T-j at bottom of hill by Hopebeck Farm turn **L** 'Scale Hill, Buttermere'. Follow road downhill, ignoring road / bridleway to left on right-hand bend.

14 At T-j with B5289 turn **L** 'Buttermere 4' then after ¼ mile first **L** (same sign). Busier section.

15 Follow for 4½ miles into Buttermere, passing Crummock Water. Shortly after Bridge Hotel climb steeply then turn first **L** 'Keswick 8½'.

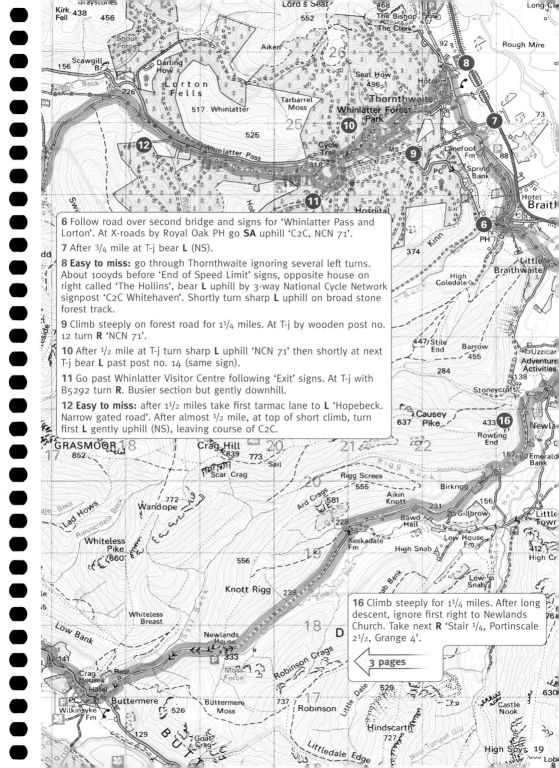

6 Follow road over second bridge and signs for 'Whinlatter Pass and Lorton'. At X-roads by Royal Oak PH go **SA** uphill 'C2C, NCN 71'.

7 After 3/4 mile at T-j bear **L** (NS).

8 Easy to miss: go through Thornthwaite ignoring several left turns. About 100yds before 'End of Speed Limit' signs, opposite house on right called 'The Hollins', bear **L** uphill by 3-way National Cycle Network signpost 'C2C Whitehaven'. Shortly turn sharp **L** uphill on broad stone forest track.

9 Climb steeply on forest road for 1¼ miles. At T-j by wooden post no. 12 turn **R** 'NCN 71'.

10 After ½ mile at T-j turn sharp **L** uphill 'NCN 71' then shortly at next T-j bear **L** past post no. 14 (same sign).

11 Go past Whinlatter Visitor Centre following 'Exit' signs. At T-j with B5292 turn **R**. Busier section but gently downhill.

12 Easy to miss: after 1½ miles take first tarmac lane to **L** 'Hopebeck. Narrow gated road'. After almost ½ mile, at top of short climb, turn first **L** gently uphill (NS), leaving course of C2C.

16 Climb steeply for 1¼ miles. After long descent, ignore first right to Newlands Church. Take next **R** 'Stair ¼, Portinscale 2½, Grange 4'.

3 pages

A tour of Skiddaw from Keswick

Although Keswick is one of the most popular tourist spots in the Lake District, you soon leave the crowds behind on this ride as you glide away from Keswick on a 3-mile section of railway path through lovely woodland, crossing and recrossing the River Greta, at one point using an extraordinary cantilevered wooden section above the valley floor. The railway path neatly links to a segregated cyclepath alongside the A66 which in turn leads to the start of the wonderful quiet gated lane running along the base of the great massif of Blencathra. North of Mungrisdale the unfenced road runs over the open

fellside, passing remote farms with the hills of Bowscale Fell and Carrock Fells constant companions to the west. The closely spaced settlements of Hesket Newmarket and Caldbeck both offer a variety of refreshments. The pub in Hesket Newmarket is owned and run by the community. John Peel of hunting fame ('Do ye ken John Peel with his coat so grey?') was buried at Caldbeck after falling from his horse in 1854 aged 78. The river-powered woollen mills once produced grey cloth for Peel's hunting

coats. The longest climb of the day follows Caldbeck, up onto Aughertree Fell with ever better views of the Ulldale Fells and the back of Skiddaw to the south. The beautiful old ornate façade of the house at Orthwaite is one of the highlights as you drop down from the moorland to a more lush and wooded landscape. There is an unavoidable 2-mile section on the A591 before you turn off to Applethwaite and some of the best views of the day towards the fells surrounding Derwent Water.

Overview

33 miles / 53 kilometres ● Moderate

Start
Keswick Leisure Pool, on Brundholme Road, signposted off the A5271 on the north side of Keswick (near the A66 roundabout)

Parking
As above

Busy roads
About 2 miles on the A591 to the west of Keswick, near the end of the ride **17** to **18**

Terrain
Gentle gradients on first half of ride. Hillier with longer climbs on second half. Longest climb - 425ft (130m) west of Caldbeck

Nearest railway
Penrith or Wigton

Refreshments
Keswick
Lots of choice

Threlkeld
Horse & Farrier PH
T: 017687 79688
Salutation Inn
T: 017687 79614

Mungrisdale
Mill Inn
T: 017687 79632

Hesket Newmarket
Old Crown PH
T: 016974 78288
Tearoom
T: 016974 78229

Caldbeck
Watermill Café
T: 016974 78267
Oddfellows Arms PH
T: 016974 78227
Old Smithy Tearoom
T: 016974 78246

Bassenthwaite
Sun Inn
T: 017687 76439

Other rides nearby

Ride 3

Ride 2
Page 14

Map pages

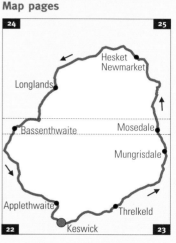

24 · 25
Hesket Newmarket
Longlands
Bassenthwaite · Mosedale
Mungrisdale
Applethwaite · Threlkeld
22 · Keswick · 23

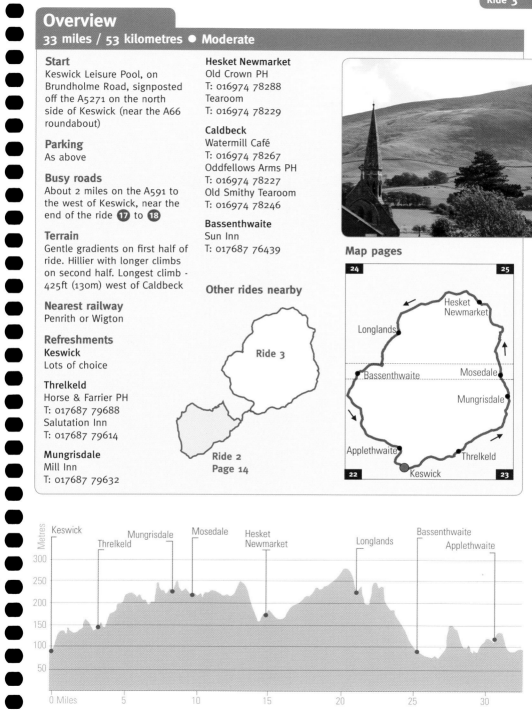

Keswick
Threlkeld
Mungrisdale
Mosedale
Hesket Newmarket
Longlands
Bassenthwaite
Applethwaite

Metres
300
250
200
150
100
50

0 Miles   5   10   15   20   25   30

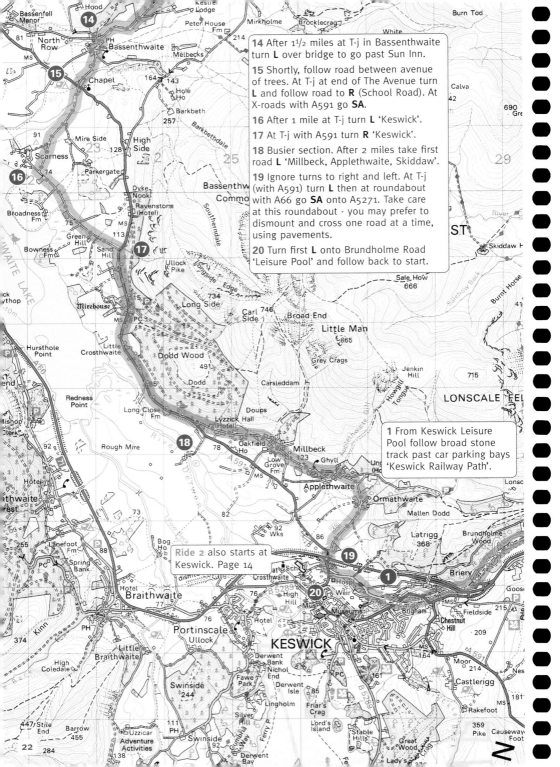

14 After 1¹/₂ miles at T-j in Bassenthwaite turn **L** over bridge to go past Sun Inn.

15 Shortly, follow road between avenue of trees. At T-j at end of The Avenue turn **L** and follow road to **R** (School Road). At X-roads with A591 go **SA**.

16 After 1 mile at T-j turn **L** 'Keswick'.

17 At T-j with A591 turn **R** 'Keswick'.

18 Busier section. After 2 miles take first road **L** 'Millbeck, Applethwaite, Skiddaw'.

19 Ignore turns to right and left. At T-j (with A591) turn **L** then at roundabout with A66 go **SA** onto A5271. Take care at this roundabout - you may prefer to dismount and cross one road at a time, using pavements.

20 Turn first **L** onto Brundholme Road 'Leisure Pool' and follow back to start.

1 From Keswick Leisure Pool follow broad stone track past car parking bays 'Keswick Railway Path'.

Ride 2 also starts at Keswick. Page 14

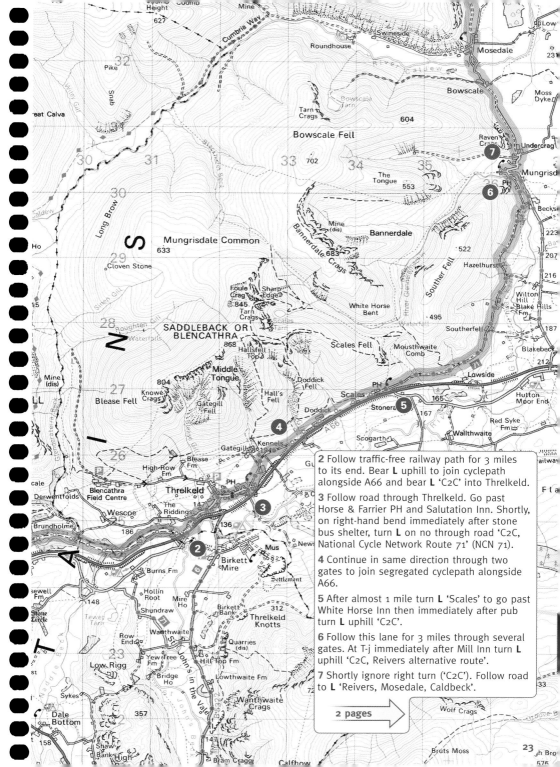

2 Follow traffic-free railway path for 3 miles to its end. Bear **L** uphill to join cyclepath alongside A66 and bear **L** 'C2C' into Threlkeld.

3 Follow road through Threlkeld. Go past Horse & Farrier PH and Salutation Inn. Shortly, on right-hand bend immediately after stone bus shelter, turn **L** on no through road 'C2C, National Cycle Network Route 71' (NCN 71).

4 Continue in same direction through two gates to join segregated cyclepath alongside A66.

5 After almost 1 mile turn **L** 'Scales' to go past White Horse Inn then immediately after pub turn **L** uphill 'C2C'.

6 Follow this lane for 3 miles through several gates. At T-j immediately after Mill Inn turn **L** uphill 'C2C, Reivers alternative route'.

7 Shortly ignore right turn ('C2C'). Follow road to **L** 'Reivers, Mosedale, Caldbeck'.

2 pages →

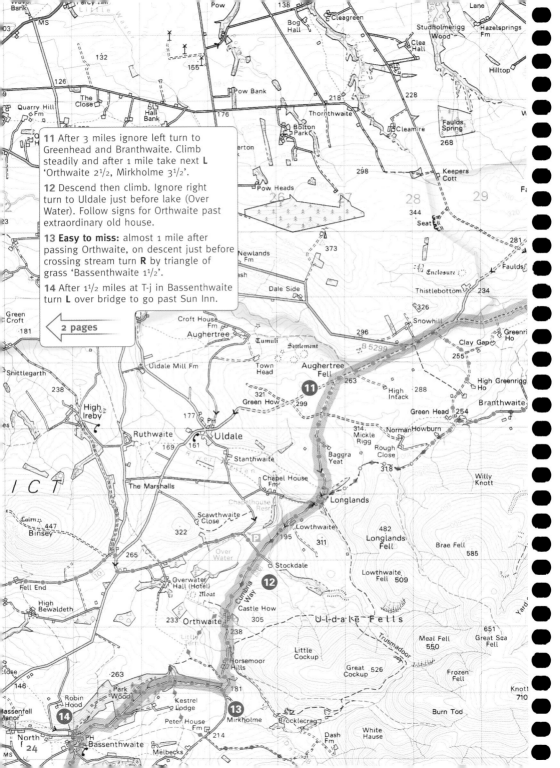

11 After 3 miles ignore left turn to Greenhead and Branthwaite. Climb steadily and after 1 mile take next **L** 'Orthwaite 2½, Mirkholme 3½'.

12 Descend then climb. Ignore right turn to Uldale just before lake (Over Water). Follow signs for Orthwaite past extraordinary old house.

13 **Easy to miss:** almost 1 mile after passing Orthwaite, on descent just before crossing stream turn **R** by triangle of grass 'Bassenthwaite 1½'.

14 After 1½ miles at T-j in Bassenthwaite turn **L** over bridge to go past Sun Inn.

← **2 pages**

8 After almost 3 miles ignore left turn (NS). At T-j after further $2\frac{1}{4}$ miles turn **R** 'Hesket Newmarket $1\frac{1}{4}$, Caldbeck 3'.

9 At T-j after 1 mile turn **L** 'Hesket Newmarket $\frac{1}{2}$, Caldbeck 2'.

10 Go through Caldbeck ignoring right turns. Follow B5299 towards Uldale and Keswick.

Shap, Haweswater & Crosby Ravensworth

S hap used to be a staging post on the A6 as coaches and horses made their way north up to Scotland and there are signs of the old stables along both sides of the main street through the village. The ride climbs from Shap up to Haweswater on the old concrete road that was used by construction vehicles on their way up to the reservoir, built in the early 20th century to provide water for Manchester. The natural catchment area for Haweswater is small, so additional water is piped into the reservoir from the adjoining valleys and is

topped up by as much as 100 million litres a day from Ullswater. At the end of the construction road you have the option of a side trip to visit Haweswater. This is highly recommended, certainly as far as the dam and best of all right to the end of the tarmac for some of the most dramatic views. Heading north from Haweswater along the valley there are chances of coffee and pub stops in both Bampton and Askham. Descend to cross the River Lowther before climbing past the dramatic outline of Lowther Castle. Only the fairy-tale façade of towers, turrets and battlements remain of the 19th-century building as the interior was dismantled in 1957, judged too expensive

to run. Cross the A6 and M6 then descend through the village of Morland (pub and café) to the lovely valley of the River Lyvennet. This is followed south, climbing gently through King's Meaburn and Maulds Meaburn. Following the rebellion of Hugh de Morville (Lord of the Manor of Meaburn) in 1173, his lands were confiscated by King Henry II. Henry granted half the manor to Hugh's sister Maud and retained the other half - King's Meaburn in the Barony of Westmorland. In Crosby Ravensworth the ride turns west for the steepest climb of the day, rewarded by excellent views of the fells ahead and a superb fast descent back down to Shap.

Overview

30 miles / 48 kilometres ● Moderate

Optional 10 mile / 16km extension to the end of Haweswater

Start
Centre of Shap, on the A6
north of Kendal

Parking
Free car park along the main
street

Busy roads
Two very short sections of A6
through Shap ① and ㉒

Terrain
Undulating in the first half of
the ride. One long gentle climb
(655ft / 200m) over several
miles starts after crossing the
River Lyvennet east of Morland
and reaches the summit
between Crosby Ravensworth
and Shap

Nearest railway
Penrith

Refreshments
Shap
Lots of choice

Haweswater
Haweswater Hotel
T: 01931 713235

Bampton
Tea room at village store
T: 01931 713351
Mardale Inn
T: 01931 713244

Bampton Grange
Crown & Mitre PH
T: 01931 713225

Askham
Queens Head PH
T: 01931 712225
Café at village stores
T: 01931 712187

Great Strickland
Strickland Arms PH
T: 01931 712238

Morland
Crown Inn
T: 01931 714310
Mill Yard Café
T: 01931 714155

Kings Meaburn
White Horse Inn
T: 01931 714256

Crosby Ravensworth
Butchers Arms PH
T: 01931 715202

Other rides nearby

Ride 5
Page 32

Ride 4

Ride 6
Page 38

Map pages

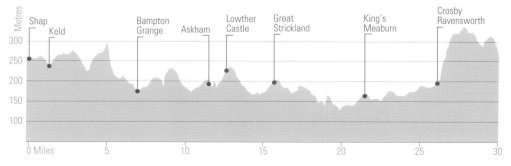

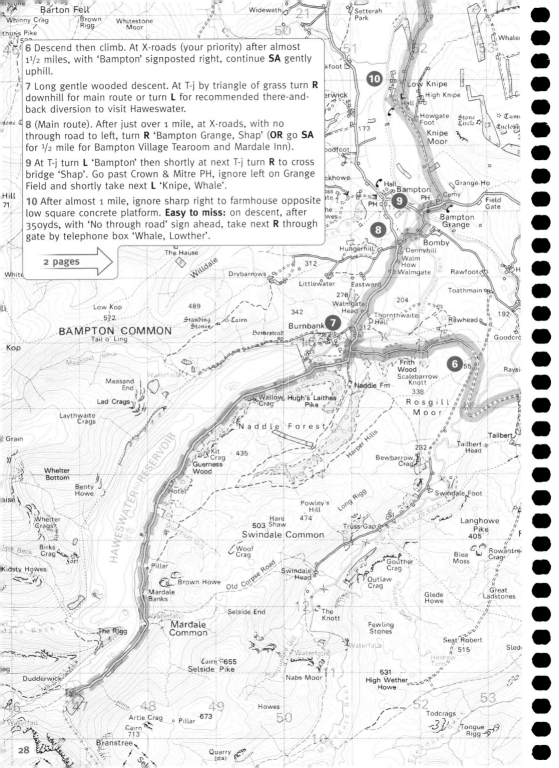

6 Descend then climb. At X-roads (your priority) after almost 1½ miles, with 'Bampton' signposted right, continue **SA** gently uphill.

7 Long gentle wooded descent. At T-j by triangle of grass turn **R** downhill for main route or turn **L** for recommended there-and-back diversion to visit Haweswater.

8 (Main route). After just over 1 mile, at X-roads, with no through road to left, turn **R** 'Bampton Grange, Shap' (**OR** go **SA** for ½ mile for Bampton Village Tearoom and Mardale Inn).

9 At T-j turn **L** 'Bampton' then shortly at next T-j turn **R** to cross bridge 'Shap'. Go past Crown & Mitre PH, ignore left on Grange Field and shortly take next **L** 'Knipe, Whale'.

10 After almost 1 mile, ignore sharp right to farmhouse opposite low square concrete platform. **Easy to miss:** on descent, after 350yds, with 'No through road' sign ahead, take next **R** through gate by telephone box 'Whale, Lowther'.

2 pages ⟹

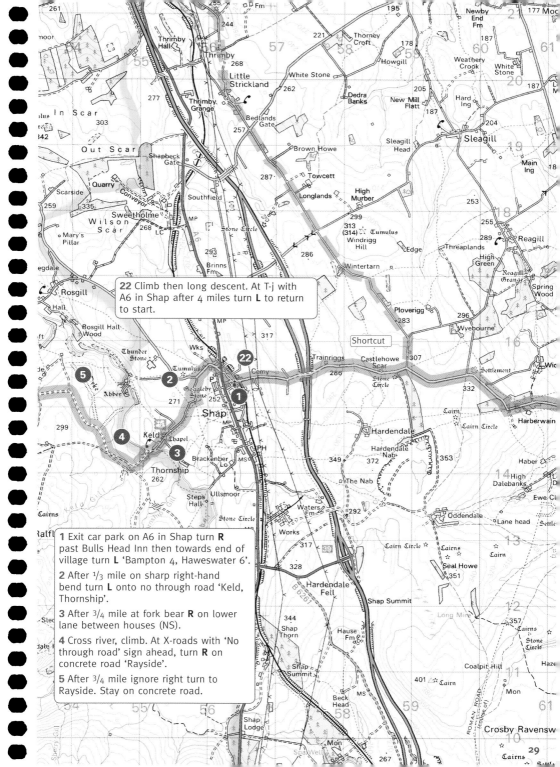

22 Climb then long descent. At T-j with A6 in Shap after 4 miles turn **L** to return to start.

Shortcut

1 Exit car park on A6 in Shap turn **R** past Bulls Head Inn then towards end of village turn **L** 'Bampton 4, Haweswater 6'.

2 After $1/3$ mile on sharp right-hand bend turn **L** onto no through road 'Keld, Thornship'.

3 After $3/4$ mile at fork bear **R** on lower lane between houses (NS).

4 Cross river, climb. At X-roads with 'No through road' sign ahead, turn **R** on concrete road 'Rayside'.

5 After $3/4$ mile ignore right turn to Rayside. Stay on concrete road.

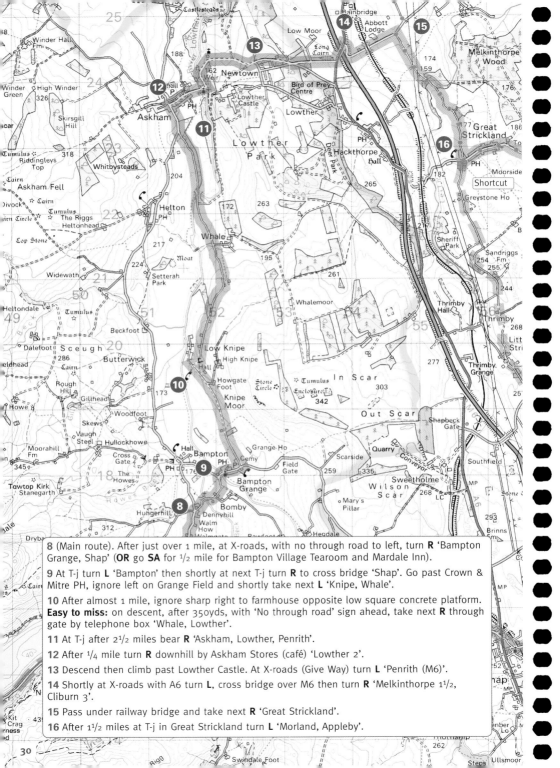

8 (Main route). After just over 1 mile, at X-roads, with no through road to left, turn **R** 'Bampton Grange, Shap' (**OR** go **SA** for ½ mile for Bampton Village Tearoom and Mardale Inn).

9 At T-j turn **L** 'Bampton' then shortly at next T-j turn **R** to cross bridge 'Shap'. Go past Crown & Mitre PH, ignore left on Grange Field and shortly take next **L** 'Knipe, Whale'.

10 After almost 1 mile, ignore sharp right to farmhouse opposite low square concrete platform. **Easy to miss:** on descent, after 350yds, with 'No through road' sign ahead, take next **R** through gate by telephone box 'Whale, Lowther'.

11 At T-j after 2½ miles bear **R** 'Askham, Lowther, Penrith'.

12 After ¼ mile turn **R** downhill by Askham Stores (café) 'Lowther 2'.

13 Descend then climb past Lowther Castle. At X-roads (Give Way) turn **L** 'Penrith (M6)'.

14 Shortly at X-roads with A6 turn **L**, cross bridge over M6 then turn **R** 'Melkinthorpe 1½, Cliburn 3'.

15 Pass under railway bridge and take next **R** 'Great Strickland'.

16 After 1½ miles at T-j in Great Strickland turn **L** 'Morland, Appleby'.

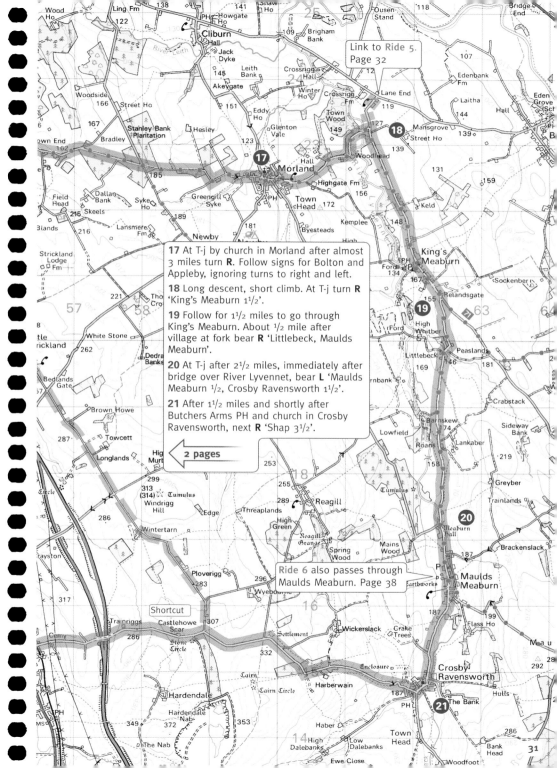

Link to **Ride** 5.
Page 32

17 At T-j by church in Morland after almost 3 miles turn **R**. Follow signs for Bolton and Appleby, ignoring turns to right and left.

18 Long descent, short climb. At T-j turn **R** 'King's Meaburn 1½'.

19 Follow for 1½ miles to go through King's Meaburn. About ½ mile after village at fork bear **R** 'Littlebeck, Maulds Meaburn'.

20 At T-j after 2½ miles, immediately after bridge over River Lyvennet, bear **L** 'Maulds Meaburn ½, Crosby Ravensworth 1½'.

21 After 1½ miles and shortly after Butchers Arms PH and church in Crosby Ravensworth, next **R** 'Shap 3½'.

◄ **2 pages**

Ride 6 also passes through Maulds Meaburn. Page 38

Shortcut

Appleby along the base of the Pennines

Appleby is one of those attractive towns that is an ideal base - it is large enough to offer a good variety of pubs, cafés and accommodation and, from a cycling perspective, there are good networks of quiet lanes extending in all directions, east and west along the valley of the River Eden, southwest over the fells to the upper Lune valley or, in this case, northwest along the base of the Pennines with dramatic views towards oddly shaped hills and steep-sided valleys. Many of the buildings in Appleby and along the ride are made of distinctive red sandstone: on your way

south out of town you pass the bare exposed rock right alongside the road. The gentle wooded climb alongside Hilton Beck heads straight towards the Pennines and the start of the delightful lane running northwest at the base of the hills. To the east there is no road for 10 miles until you reach the B6277 high in upper Teesdale. The evocatively named Roman Fell, Mell Fell, Murton Pike and Middle Tongue come in all shapes and sizes, cut through by deep valleys such as Scordale, Gasdale and High Cup Gill. Continue northwest through Dufton with its unusual round-topped

memorial and the hamlets of Knock, Milburn and Blencarn to Kirkland and one of the most unlikely place names you will find on an Ordnance Survey map: 'The Hanging Walls of Mark Anthony' (!) The exotic name is given to strip lynchets or cultivation terraces now largely grassed over. The ride turns south at Skirwith and drops down into the Eden Valley beyond Culgaith (divert off the route here for a good tea stop at Acorn Bank, a National Trust property). The River Eden is crossed to the south of Temple Sowerby and undulating lanes are followed back through Bolton and Colby into Appleby.

Overview

30 miles / 48 kilometres ● Easy / Moderate

Start
Tourist Information Centre, High Street, Appleby in Westmorland

Parking
Several car parks in Appleby

Busy roads
None

Terrain
Long steady climb (460ft / 140m) at the start then gently undulating

Nearest railway
Appleby

Other rides nearby

Refreshments
Appleby in Westmorland
Lots of choice

Dufton
Stag Inn
T: 017683 51608

Culgaith
Black Swan PH
T: 01768 88223

Acorn Bank (National Trust)
Tearoom
T: 017683 61893

Temple Sowerby
Kings Arms Hotel
T: 017683 61211

Bolton
Eden Vale Inn
T: 01768 361428

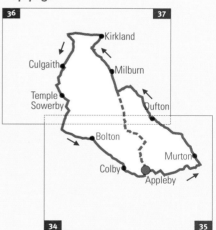

Map pages

Ride 5

Ride 4
Page 26

Ride 6
Page 38

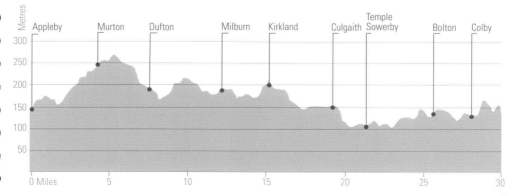

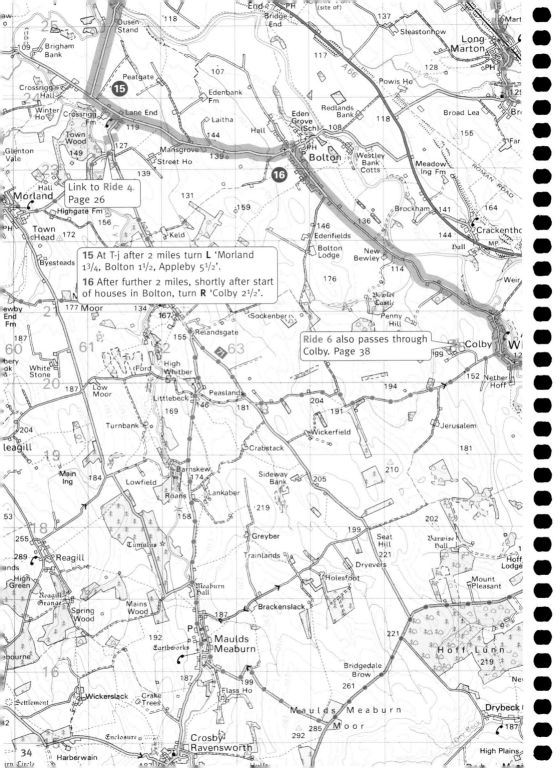

Link to **Ride 4**. Page 26

15 At T-j after 2 miles turn **L** 'Morland 1¾, Bolton 1½, Appleby 5½'.

16 After further 2 miles, shortly after start of houses in Bolton, turn **R** 'Colby 2½'.

Ride 6 also passes through Colby. Page 38

34

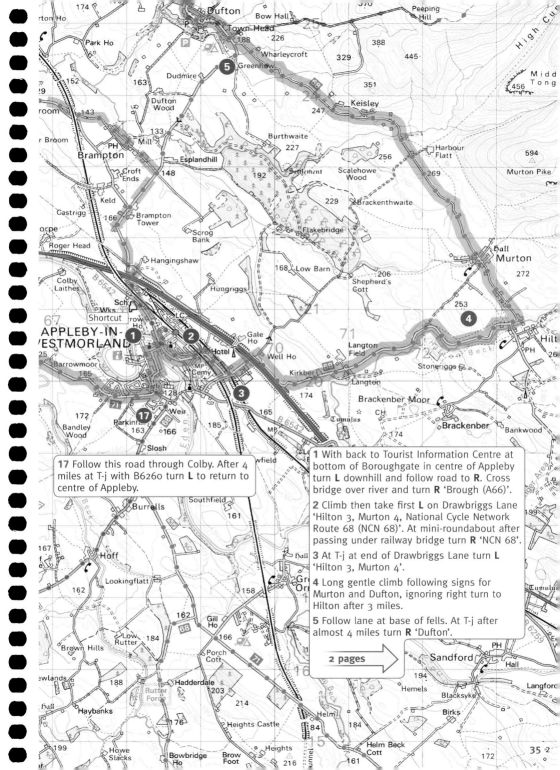

17 Follow this road through Colby. After 4 miles at T-j with B6260 turn **L** to return to centre of Appleby.

1 With back to Tourist Information Centre at bottom of Boroughgate in centre of Appleby turn **L** downhill and follow road to **R**. Cross bridge over river and turn **R** 'Brough (A66)'.

2 Climb then take first **L** on Drawbriggs Lane 'Hilton 3, Murton 4, National Cycle Network Route 68 (NCN 68)'. At mini-roundabout after passing under railway bridge turn **R** 'NCN 68'.

3 At T-j at end of Drawbriggs Lane turn **L** 'Hilton 3, Murton 4'.

4 Long gentle climb following signs for Murton and Dufton, ignoring right turn to Hilton after 3 miles.

5 Follow lane at base of fells. At T-j after almost 4 miles turn **R** 'Dufton'.

2 pages ➡

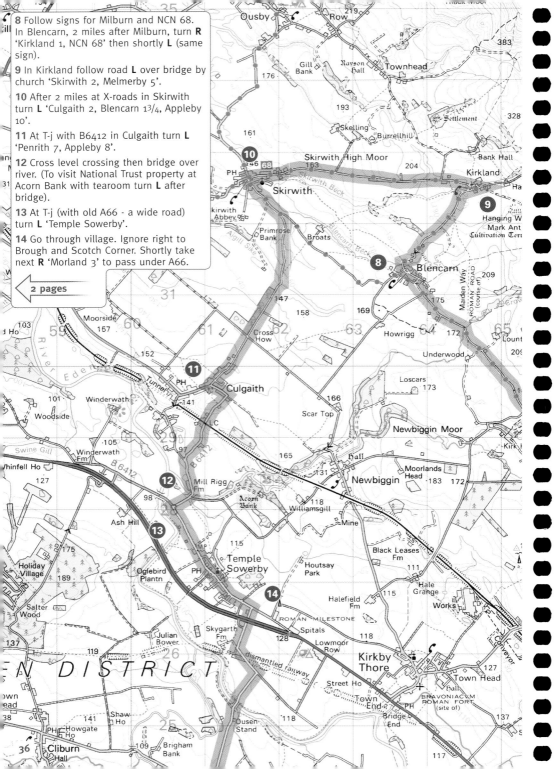

8 Follow signs for Milburn and NCN 68. In Blencarn, 2 miles after Milburn, turn **R** 'Kirkland 1, NCN 68' then shortly **L** (same sign).

9 In Kirkland follow road **L** over bridge by church 'Skirwith 2, Melmerby 5'.

10 After 2 miles at X-roads in Skirwith turn **L** 'Culgaith 2, Blencarn 1¾, Appleby 10'.

11 At T-j with B6412 in Culgaith turn **L** 'Penrith 7, Appleby 8'.

12 Cross level crossing then bridge over river. (To visit National Trust property at Acorn Bank with tearoom turn **L** after bridge).

13 At T-j (with old A66 - a wide road) turn **L** 'Temple Sowerby'.

14 Go through village. Ignore right to Brough and Scotch Corner. Shortly take next **R** 'Morland 3' to pass under A66.

2 pages

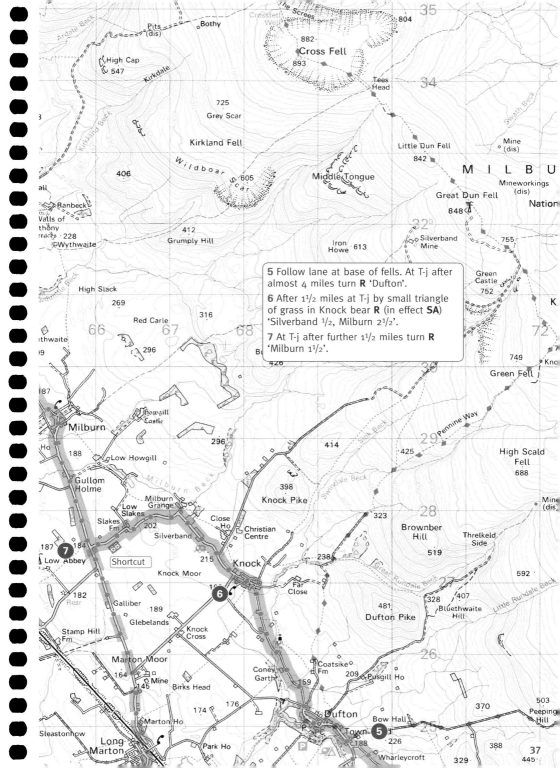

5 Follow lane at base of fells. At T-j after almost 4 miles turn **R** 'Dufton'.

6 After 1¹/₂ miles at T-j by small triangle of grass in Knock bear **R** (in effect **SA**) 'Silverband ¹/₂, Milburn 2¹/₂'.

7 At T-j after further 1¹/₂ miles turn **R** 'Milburn 1¹/₂'.

Orton to Appleby

As you emerge from the Lune Gorge, squeezed between the Howgill Fells to the east and the Shap Fells to the west, Orton is one of the first villages that you come to as the valley widens out. It is a fine little place with a pub, chocolate factory with attached tearoom, a good supply of home-made cakes in the village shop and a monthly Farmers' Market. To the north lie the limestone outcrops of Great Asby Scar. The ride heads east through Raisbeck and onto the unfenced fell road passing Sunbiggin Tarn, a favourite spot for ice skating during hard winters. Drop down from the limestone summit with fabulous views ahead

of the Pennines, rising to 2930ft (893m) on Cross Fell, the highest point in England outside the Lake District. The final section into Appleby is on the busier B6260 although most of this is downhill. Appleby is the former capital of Westmorland and is in fact two towns either side of the River Eden. The old part is the 10th-century Danish village on a bluff overlooking the 'newer' part which grew around the 12th-century Norman Castle. Nowadays it is more famous for the annual Horse Fair, drawing travellers from all over the country to buy and sell horses. There are plenty of cafés and pubs for refreshments. Head west from Appleby crossing from

the valley of the Eden to the valley of the River Lyvennet, soon passing through Maulds Meaburn and Crosby Ravensworth. The church here is large enough to be called 'a cathedral in miniature' complete with gargoyles and ornate stone carvings. The long steady climb up to the top of Orton Scar leaves you with one of the fastest descents you are ever likely to enjoy as you return to Orton.

Overview

27 miles / 43 kilometres ● Moderate

Start
Orton, 3 miles north of M6 Jct 38

Parking
On street parking

Busy roads
● The B6260 into Appleby **6** to **7**

● The B6260 back into Orton (a fast downhill) **13** to **14**

Terrain
Two main climbs, the first at the start past Sunbiggin Tarn (330ft / 100m) and the second south from Maulds Meaburn to Orton Scar (570ft / 175m). Several shorter climbs

Nearest railway
Appleby

Refreshments
Orton
George Hotel
T: 01539 624229
Chocolate Factory tearoom
T: 01539 624781

Great Asby (just off the route)
Three Greyhounds PH
T: 017683 51428

Appleby in Westmorland
Lots of choice

Crosby Ravensworth
Butchers Arms PH
T: 01931 715202

Other rides nearby

Ride 5
Page 32

Ride 4
Page 26

Ride 6

Ride 8
Page 50

Map pages

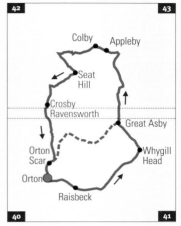

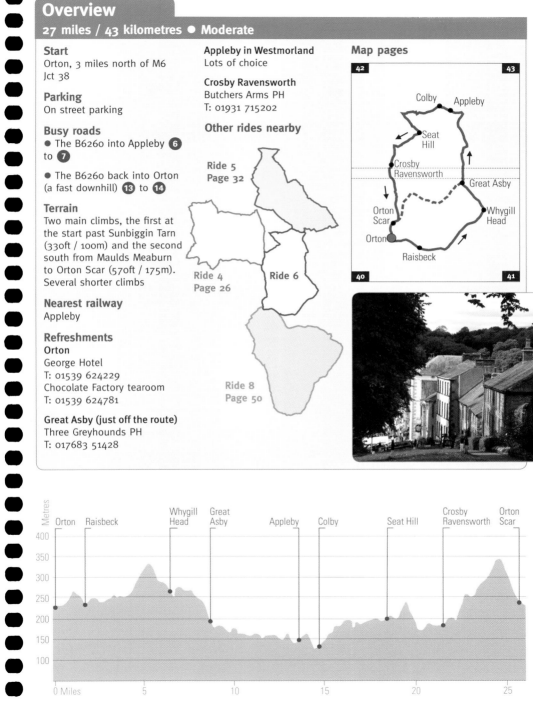

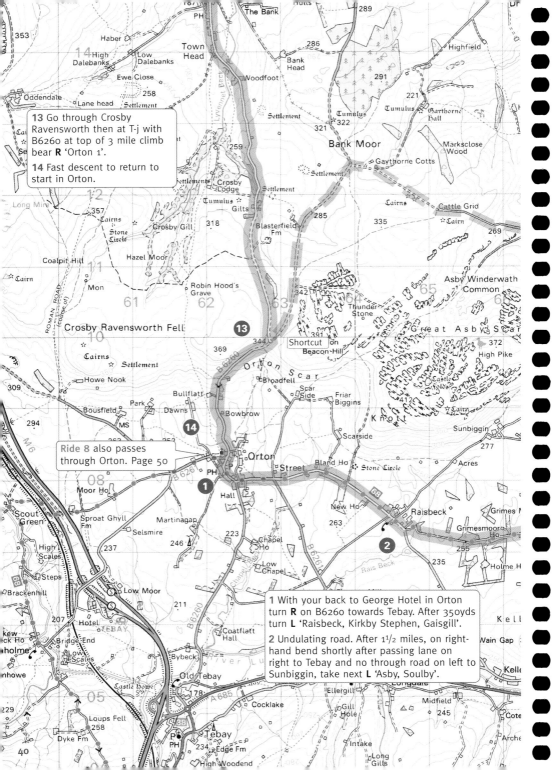

13 Go through Crosby Ravensworth then at T-j with B6260 at top of 3 mile climb bear **R** 'Orton 1'.

14 Fast descent to return to start in Orton.

Shortcut on Beacon Hill

Ride 8 also passes through Orton. Page 50

1 With your back to George Hotel in Orton turn **R** on B6260 towards Tebay. After 350yds turn **L** 'Raisbeck, Kirkby Stephen, Gaisgill'.

2 Undulating road. After 1½ miles, on right-hand bend shortly after passing lane on right to Tebay and no through road on left to Sunbiggin, take next **L** 'Asby, Soulby'.

40

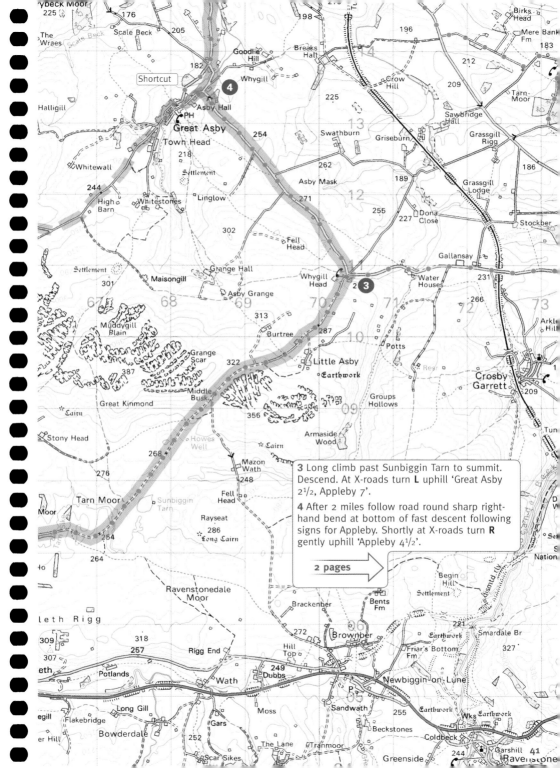

3 Long climb past Sunbiggin Tarn to summit. Descend. At X-roads turn **L** uphill 'Great Asby 2¹/₂, Appleby 7'.

4 After 2 miles follow road round sharp right-hand bend at bottom of fast descent following signs for Appleby. Shortly at X-roads turn **R** gently uphill 'Appleby 4¹/₂'.

2 pages ➡

41

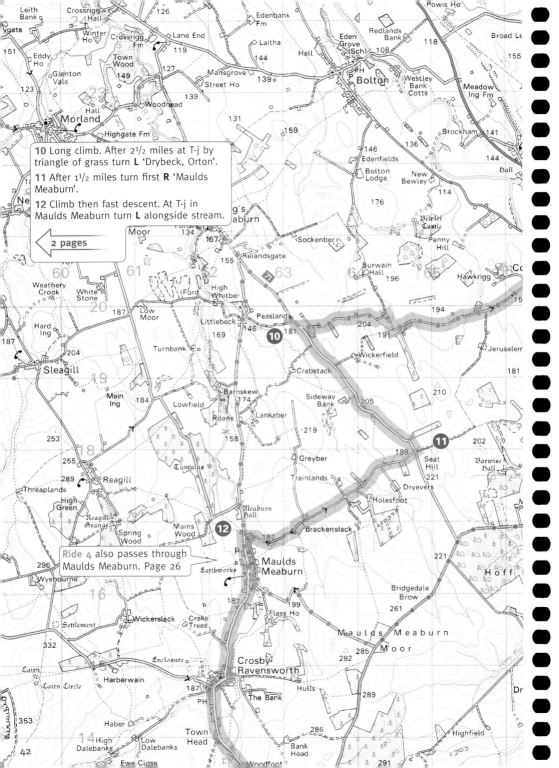

10 Long climb. After 2¹/₂ miles at T-j by triangle of grass turn **L** 'Drybeck, Orton'.

11 After 1¹/₂ miles turn first **R** 'Maulds Meaburn'.

12 Climb then fast descent. At T-j in Maulds Meaburn turn **L** alongside stream.

← **2 pages**

Ride 4 also passes through Maulds Meaburn. Page 26

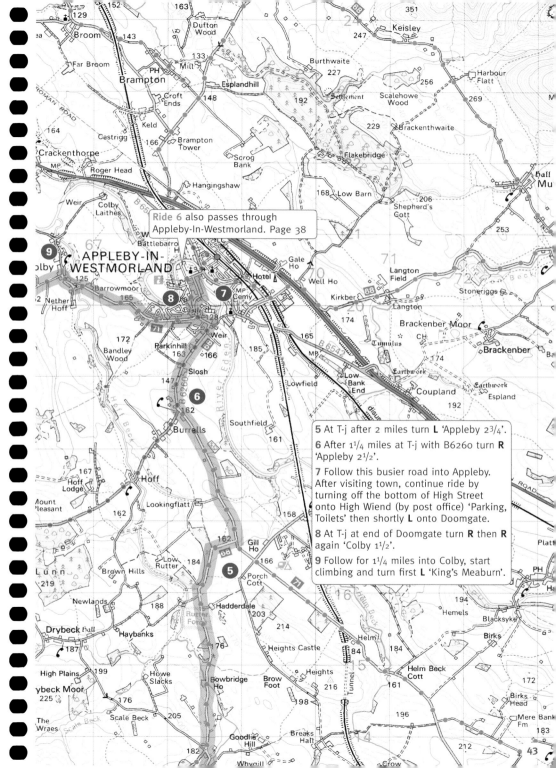

Ride 6 also passes through Appleby-In-Westmorland. Page 38

5 At T-j after 2 miles turn **L** 'Appleby 2³/₄'.

6 After 1¹/₄ miles at T-j with B6260 turn **R** 'Appleby 2¹/₂'.

7 Follow this busier road into Appleby. After visiting town, continue ride by turning off the bottom of High Street onto High Wiend (by post office) 'Parking, Toilets' then shortly **L** onto Doomgate.

8 At T-j at end of Doomgate turn **R** then **R** again 'Colby 1¹/₂'.

9 Follow for 1¹/₄ miles into Colby, start climbing and turn first **L** 'King's Meaburn'.

Kirkby Stephen, Brough & Tan Hill

The Tan Hill Inn, just inside North Yorkshire but close to the boundaries of both Durham and Cumbria, is the highest inn in England, set at 1732ft (528m) above sea level. Its existence is explained by the fact that coal was mined in the area from the 12th century to the early 20th century and the miners needed their drink! The ride takes a circuitous route to climb to Tan Hill, at first heading northeast to Soulby, passing some humorous verse painted in white on metal plates by the farm at Stripes. One about rain: '..*Next day was also fairly dry / Save for the deluge from the sky / Which wetted the party to the skin / And after that the rain set in'*. Meander north through Little and Great Musgrave, crossing Scandal Beck and the River Eden on your way to Brough. The castle was built by the Normans on the site of a Roman fort then rebuilt in medieval style. Great prosperity came to Brough in the 18th and 19th centuries with up to 60 stage coaches a day halting here on their way from London to Carlisle and on to Glasgow, or from York to Lancaster. Seventeen inns attended their needs

but decline set in when the railway was built. Half-hidden streets and a subway provide a safe exit from Brough and the start of the long climb up to Tan Hill. This climb has a few false summits so be prepared for these. The ride is a tale of three watersheds: a raindrop in Kirkby Stephen ends up in the Solway Firth, via the River Eden; one falling on the north side of Tan Hill eventually joins the Tees

and ends up in Hartlepool whereas one to the south of the pub joins the River Swale and makes its way to the North Sea at Hull! Descend from moorland to the wooded delights of Swaledale before the final climb of the ride up to the Yorkshire / Cumbria county boundary. Beware of dim sheep throwing themselves under your wheels on the descent!

Overview
32 miles / 52 kilometres ● Strenuous

Start
Tourist Information Centre, Kirkby Stephen

Parking
Free car park by school

Busy roads
Generally quiet but the roads from Brough to Tan Hill and back to Kirkby Stephen will be busier in peak season / school holidays

Terrain
Hilly! First major climb from Brough to Tan Hill (1180 ft / 360m); second major climb from near Keld to highpoint on B6270 Nateby road (640ft / 195m). Several shorter climbs

Nearest railway
Kirkby Stephen (about 2 miles southwest of town)

Refreshments
Kirkby Stephen
Lots of choice

Brough
Lots of choice

Tan Hill
Tan Hill Inn
T: 01833 628246

Keld (just off route)
Keld Lodge
T: 01729 830643

Nateby
Black Bull PH
T: 017683 71588

Map pages

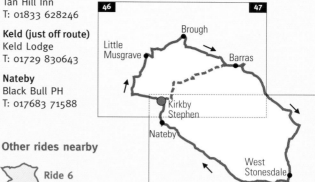

Other rides nearby

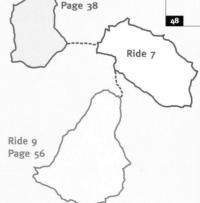

Ride 6
Page 38

Ride 7

Ride 9
Page 56

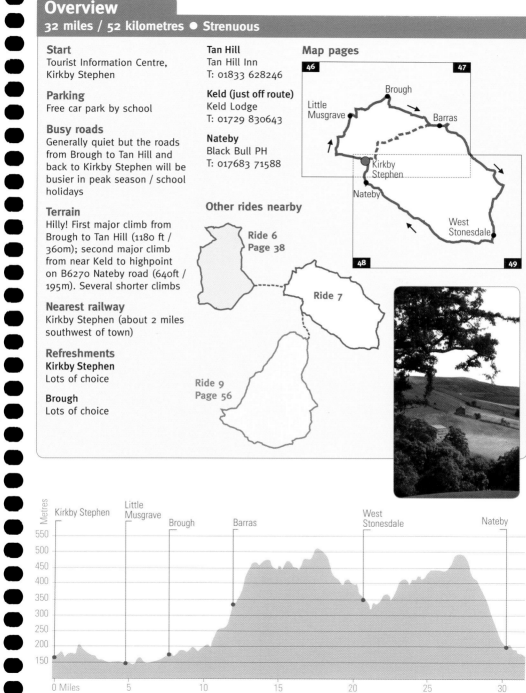

45

7 At T-j in Little Musgrave turn **R** 'Great Musgrave, Kirkby Stephen' then after almost 1/2 mile at T-j with B6259 turn **L** 'Great Musgrave 1, Warcop 2'.

8 Cross bridge over River Eden, climb, then on sharp left-hand bend turn **R** 'Great Musgrave 1/4, Brough 2'.

9 Ignore turns to right and left. At T-j shortly after crossing bridge over A66 turn **R** 'Brough 1/4, Appleby 8'.

10 At clocktower / Golden Fleece PH in Brough turn **R** 'Kirkby Stephen'.

11 Easy to miss: pass through subway under A66 then turn **R** downhill between wooden railings located to left of slip road going towards Penrith. Descend on tarmac path to join 'hidden' road.

12 After 1/2 mile, as tarmac turns to track, turn **L** through subway beneath A685 to join lane opposite (to South Stainmore).

5 Easy to miss: shortly after passing farm with interesting poems on display, at X-roads of tiny lanes (your priority) turn **R** 'Soulby, Musgrave'.

6 At T-j bear **L** gently uphill (NS) then shortly after crossing bridge over river in Soulby turn **R** 'Little Musgrave 13/4, Great Musgrave 21/2' (**NB** not road immediately after bridge).

1 From Tourist Information Centre in Kirkby Stephen head north on A685 towards Brough.

2 At mini-roundabout at end of Market Street turn **L** on Silver Street 'Soulby 2, Crosby Garrett 4'.

3 After 300yds, on right-hand bend by Kirkby Stephen Grammar School, bear **L** 'Waitby 13/4, Smardale 21/2'.

4 Descend, cross bridge over stream then at fork bear **R** 'Moorlands, Stripes, Smardale Mill'.

Link to Ride 6. Page 38

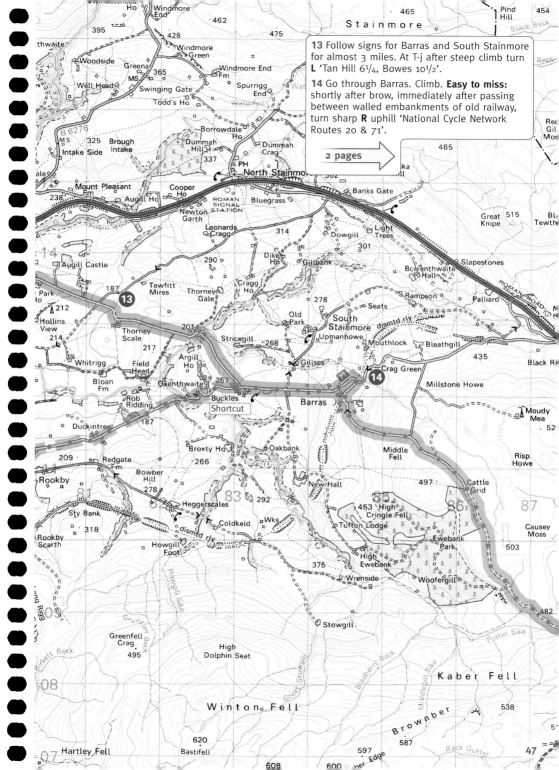

13 Follow signs for Barras and South Stainmore for almost 3 miles. At T-j after steep climb turn **L** 'Tan Hill $6\frac{1}{4}$, Bowes $10\frac{1}{2}$'.

14 Go through Barras. Climb. **Easy to miss:** shortly after brow, immediately after passing between walled embankments of old railway, turn sharp **R** uphill 'National Cycle Network Routes 20 & 71'.

2 pages →

Shortcut

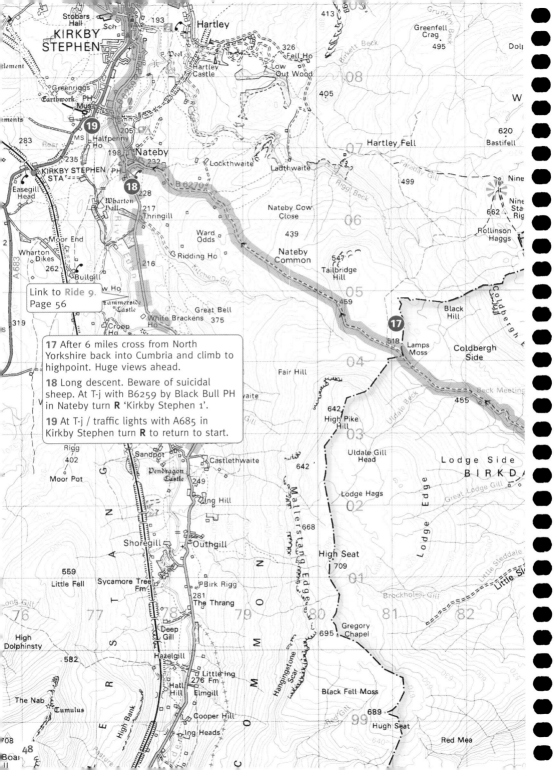

KIRKBY STEPHEN

Hartley

Stobars Hall

Sch

193

Peel

Greenfell Crag
495

Dol

326

Fell Ho

Hartley Castle

Low Out Wood

405

413

W

Greenriggs PH

Earthwork

Mus

413

08

settlement

ments

283

205

MS

Halfpenny Ho

198

Nateby

235

232

Lockthwaite

Ladthwaite

620

Bastifell

Hartley Fell

07

Faraday Gill

499

Nine

(19)

(18)

KIRKBY STEPHEN STA

228

B6270

Nine Sta Rig

662

Easegill Head

Wharton Hall

217

Thringill

Nateby Cow Close

06

Rollinson Haggs

Riggl Beck

2

Moor End

Wharton Dikes

262

216

Ward Odds

Ridding Ho

439

Nateby Common

547

Tailbridge Hill

Bullgill

Link to **Ride 9.**
Page 56

w Ho

Cammerside Castle

Croop Ho

White Brackens

Great Bell
375

05

459

518

Black Hill

Coldbergh Side

Coldbergh

319

Ho

(17)

Lamps Moss

17 After 6 miles cross from North Yorkshire back into Cumbria and climb to highpoint. Huge views ahead.

18 Long descent. Beware of suicidal sheep. At T-j with B6259 by Black Bull PH in Nateby turn **R** 'Kirkby Stephen 1'.

19 At T-j / traffic lights with A685 in Kirkby Stephen turn **R** to return to start.

Fair Hill

waite

642

High Pike Hill

04

Uldale Gill Head

455

Beck Meeting

Uldale Beck

Rigg
402

Sandpot

Castlethwaite

Lodge Side

BIRKD

Moor Pot

Pendragon Castle

642

Lodge Hags

02

249

Ing Hill

668

Lodge Edge

Great Lodge Gill

Shoregill

Outhgill

High Seat
709

03

Brockholes Gill

Little St

Little Fell

559

Sycamore Tree Fm

281

Birk Rigg

The Thrang

01

76

77

78

79

80

81

82

High Dolphinsty

Deep Gill

Gregory Chapel

695

Red Gill

582

Hazelgill

Hall Hill

Little Ing
276 Fm

Elmgill

Black Fell Moss

The Nab

Cumulus

High Bank

Cooper Hill

Ing Heads

689

Hugh Seat

Red Mea

08

48

Boar

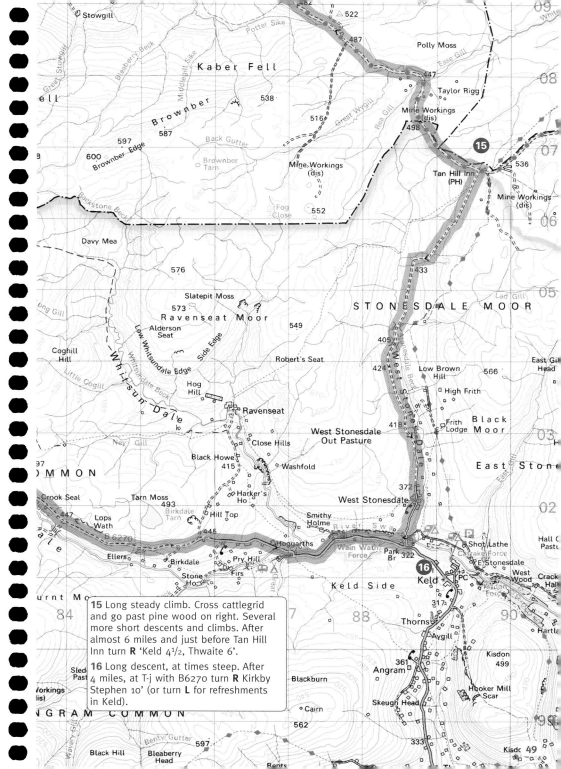

15 Long steady climb. Cross cattlegrid and go past pine wood on right. Several more short descents and climbs. After almost 6 miles and just before Tan Hill Inn turn **R** 'Keld 4½, Thwaite 6'.

16 Long descent, at times steep. After 4 miles, at T-j with B6270 turn **R** Kirkby Stephen 10' (or turn **L** for refreshments in Keld).

Sedbergh to Orton & Ravenstonedale

This ride forms a complete circuit of the Howgill Fells, the smooth grass-covered 'sleeping elephants' that rise so dramatically east of the Lune Gorge as the M6 squeezes its way through the fells between Lancaster and Penrith. There is an anomaly of the Howgills lying entirely within the Cumbria county boundary but forming part of the Yorkshire Dales National Park. Sedbergh is dominated by its school which has provided more than its fair share of England rugby players over the years. It is located right at the foot of the Howgills which form a picturesque backdrop to the town. Howgill Lane leads steeply north out of town, passing a series of stone-built farms along the east side of the Lune valley. The Lune Gorge somehow manages to accommodate the river, the M6, the West Coast Mainline, the A685 and the tiny open fell road used on this ride. There are several steep climbs and descents as you cross a series of streams tumbling down off the hillside. Cross to the west side of the river and the M6 and climb then descend to Orton, your first chance of refreshments since

leaving Sedbergh: there is a pub and a café at the chocolate factory. East of Orton the ride runs parallel with the A685 with fine views of the northern slopes of the Howgills. Ravenstonedale is a wooded sanctuary at contrast with the surrounding moorland. Climb to the Fat Lamb Inn on the A683 and

enjoy a 9-mile descent on this scenic and very quiet A road. About halfway back to Sedbergh you pass the dramatic view up the valley to Cautley Spout. Close to the road is the Cross Keys Temperance Inn which, as its name suggests, serves everything but alcohol.

Overview

33 miles / 53 kilometres ● Moderate /Strenuous

Start
Red Lion PH in the centre
of Sedbergh

Parking
Limited free parking in the long
layby on the A684 heading east
out of Sedbergh. Pay & Display
car park near the centre of
town

Busy roads
● About 1 mile on the A685
south of Tebay **5** to **6**

● About 1/2 mile on busy A685
west of Ravenstonedale **12**

● The A683 from
Ravenstonedale to Sedbergh
is rarely busy: avoid peak
summer weekends **14** to **15**

Terrain
Several climbs (some short
steep sections) on the minor
lanes north of Sedbergh to
Orton. Long gentle descent
down A683 from Fat Lamb Inn
back to Sedbergh

Nearest railway
Kirkby Stephen

Refreshments
Sedbergh
Lots of choice

Orton
George Hotel
T: 01539 624229

Chocolate Factory tearoom
T: 01539 624781

Ravenstonedale
Black Swan PH
T: 01539 623204

A683 above Ravenstonedale
Fat Lamb Inn
T: 01539 623242

Cautley
Cross Keys Temperance Inn
(tearoom, not a pub)
T: 01539 620284

Other rides nearby

Ride 6
Page 38

Ride 8

Ride 9
Page 56

Ride 10
Page 62

Map pages

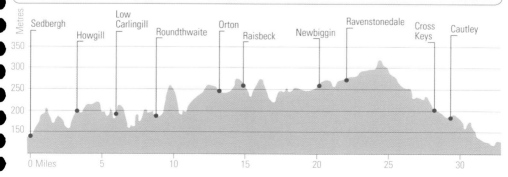

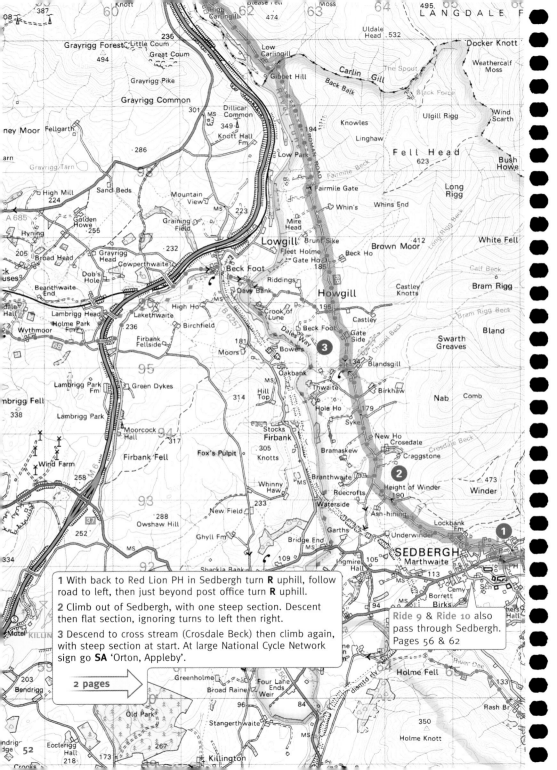

1 With back to Red Lion PH in Sedbergh turn **R** uphill, follow road to left, then just beyond post office turn **R** uphill.

2 Climb out of Sedbergh, with one steep section. Descent then flat section, ignoring turns to left then right.

3 Descend to cross stream (Crosdale Beck) then climb again, with steep section at start. At large National Cycle Network sign go **SA** 'Orton, Appleby'.

Ride 9 & Ride 10 also pass through Sedbergh. Pages 56 & 62

2 pages →

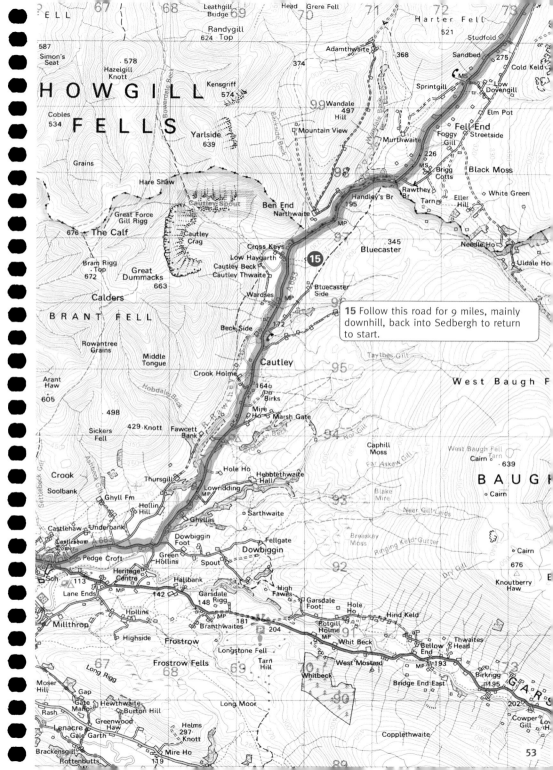

15 Follow this road for 9 miles, mainly downhill, back into Sedbergh to return to start.

53

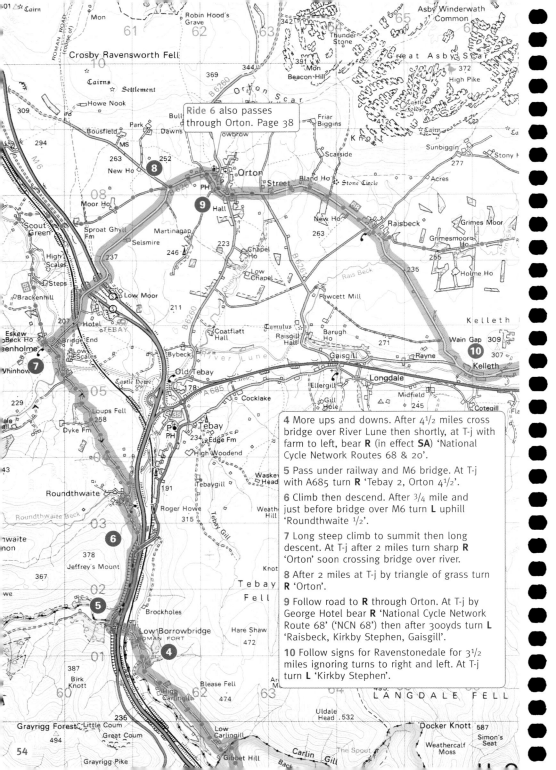

Ride 6 also passes through Orton. Page 38

4 More ups and downs. After 4¹/₂ miles cross bridge over River Lune then shortly, at T-j with farm to left, bear **R** (in effect **SA**) 'National Cycle Network Routes 68 & 20'.

5 Pass under railway and M6 bridge. At T-j with A685 turn **R** 'Tebay 2, Orton 4¹/₂'.

6 Climb then descend. After ³/₄ mile and just before bridge over M6 turn **L** uphill 'Roundthwaite ¹/₂'.

7 Long steep climb to summit then long descent. At T-j after 2 miles turn sharp **R** 'Orton' soon crossing bridge over river.

8 After 2 miles at T-j by triangle of grass turn **R** 'Orton'.

9 Follow road to **R** through Orton. At T-j by George Hotel bear **R** 'National Cycle Network Route 68' ('NCN 68') then after 300yds turn **L** 'Raisbeck, Kirkby Stephen, Gaisgill'.

10 Follow signs for Ravenstonedale for 3¹/₂ miles ignoring turns to right and left. At T-j turn **L** 'Kirkby Stephen'.

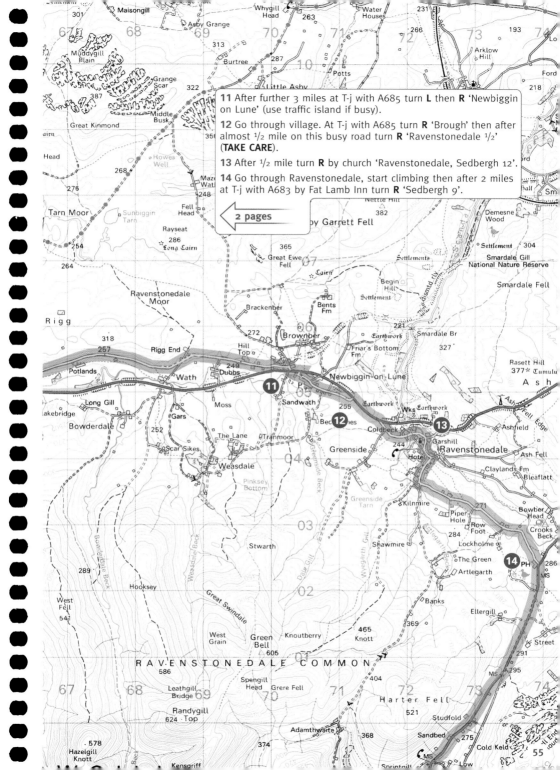

11 After further 3 miles at T-j with A685 turn **L** then **R** 'Newbiggin on Lune' (use traffic island if busy).

12 Go through village. At T-j with A685 turn **R** 'Brough' then after almost ½ mile on this busy road turn **R** 'Ravenstonedale ½' (**TAKE CARE**).

13 After ½ mile turn **R** by church 'Ravenstonedale, Sedbergh 12'.

14 Go through Ravenstonedale, start climbing then after 2 miles at T-j with A683 by Fat Lamb Inn turn **R** 'Sedbergh 9'.

2 pages

Sedbergh via Dent Station to Ravenstonedale

S edbergh has reinvented itself in the past few years as a book town with many second-hand bookshops and regular literary events. It is also famous for its public school, many of whose buildings are spread throughout the town. Head south then east from Sedbergh on the road that gradually climbs up through Dentdale to the pretty village of Dent with a short section of cobbled street to rattle your bones. Born in Dent in 1785, Adam Sedgwick is regarded as one of the founders of modern geology and there is a stone memorial to him in the centre of the village. As you follow the River Dee east from Dent towards Cowgill you may notice that it appears and disappears - not an unusual

occurrence in this limestone scenery. It has been a steady climb of about 360ft (110m) from Sedbergh up to Cowgill. This abruptly changes as you head north towards Dent Station (on the Settle Carlisle railway line) with one of the steepest climbs in the whole book, a challenging 1030ft (315m) in little over 2 miles. What goes up must come down, and there is a long fast descent to Garsdale Head and a chance of refreshment at the Moorcock Inn. This is near one of those three-way watersheds: to the west the water drains into the Clough River which ends up in the

River Lune and Morecambe Bay; to the east the River Ure eventually disgorges its water into the Humber at Hull and to the north, the course of this ride, you soon join the upper River Eden, heading towards Carlisle and the Solway Firth. Pass beneath Mallerstang and Wild Boar Fell, crossing and recrossing the railway line. At the ruins of 12th-century Pendragon Castle you turn west, climbing up to the A683 and setting you up for a gentle 10-mile descent back to Sedbergh, passing the Fat Lamb Inn and Cautley Spout on your way.

Overview
35 miles / 56 kilometres ● Strenuous

Start
Red Lion pub in the centre of Sedbergh

Parking
Limited free parking in the long layby on the A684 heading east out of Sedbergh. Or Pay & Display car park

Busy roads
● The A683 is one of the quietest A roads in this part of Cumbria ⑨ to ⑫

● Sedbergh to Dent is likely to be busier. Avoid peak summer weekends ① to ②

Other rides nearby

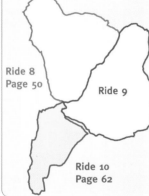

Ride 8
Page 50

Ride 9

Ride 10
Page 62

Terrain
Exceedingly steep climb from Dentdale past Dent Station (1030ft / 315m). Short steep climb west of Pendragon Castle to A683 (285ft / 85m). Several other short climbs

Nearest railway
Dent

Refreshments
Sedbergh
Lots of choice

Dent
Two pubs, two cafés

Garsdale Head
Moorcock Inn
T: 01969 667488

A683 above Ravenstonedale
Fat Lamb Inn
T: 01539 623242

Cautley
Cross Keys Temperance Inn (tearoom, not a pub)
T: 01539 620284

Map pages

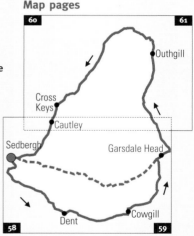

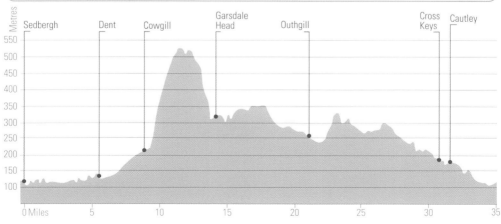

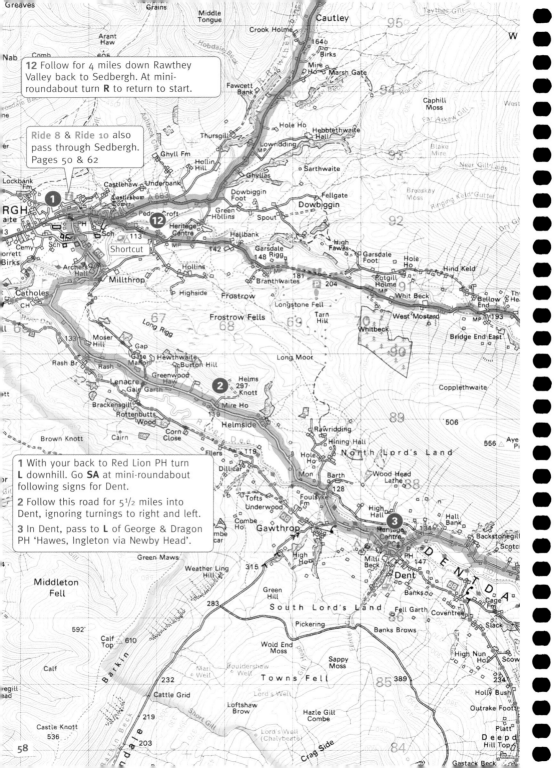

12 Follow for 4 miles down Rawthey Valley back to Sedbergh. At mini-roundabout turn **R** to return to start.

Ride 8 & Ride 10 also pass through Sedbergh. Pages 50 & 62

1 With your back to Red Lion PH turn **L** downhill. Go **SA** at mini-roundabout following signs for Dent.

2 Follow this road for 5½ miles into Dent, ignoring turnings to right and left.

3 In Dent, pass to **L** of George & Dragon PH 'Hawes, Ingleton via Newby Head'.

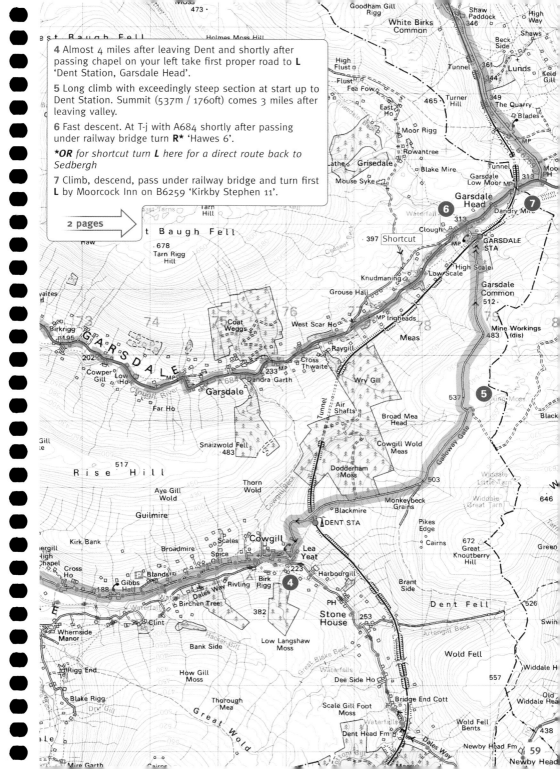

4 Almost 4 miles after leaving Dent and shortly after passing chapel on your left take first proper road to **L** 'Dent Station, Garsdale Head'.

5 Long climb with exceedingly steep section at start up to Dent Station. Summit (537m / 1760ft) comes 3 miles after leaving valley.

6 Fast descent. At T-j with A684 shortly after passing under railway bridge turn **R*** 'Hawes 6'.

***OR** for shortcut turn **L** here for a direct route back to Sedbergh*

7 Climb, descend, pass under railway bridge and turn first **L** by Moorcock Inn on B6259 'Kirkby Stephen 11'.

2 pages ➡

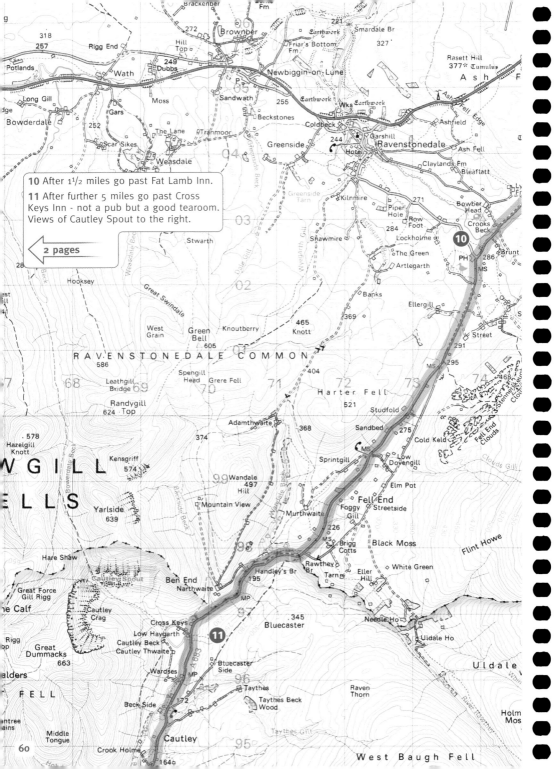

10 After 1½ miles go past Fat Lamb Inn.

11 After further 5 miles go past Cross Keys Inn - not a pub but a good tearoom. Views of Cautley Spout to the right.

◁ 2 pages

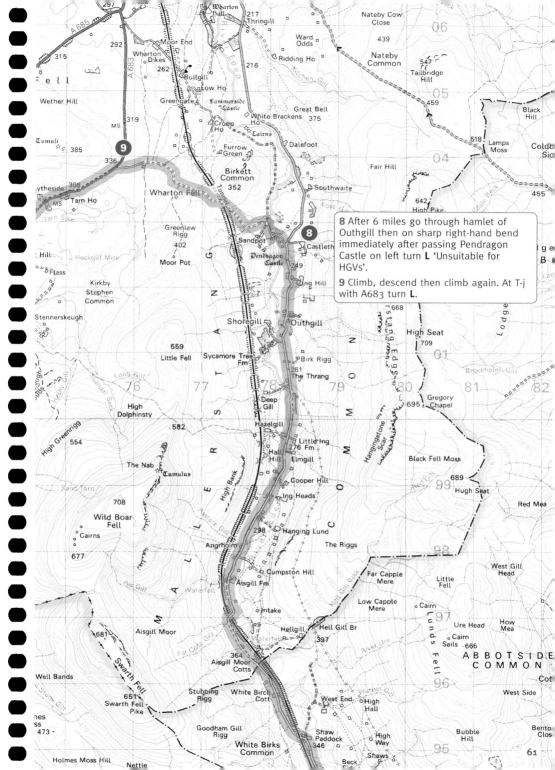

8 After 6 miles go through hamlet of Outhgill then on sharp right-hand bend immediately after passing Pendragon Castle on left turn **L** 'Unsuitable for HGVs'.

9 Climb, descend then climb again. At T-j with A683 turn **L**.

Kirkby Lonsdale to Sedbergh

Kirkby Lonsdale is the start point for three rides in the book. It is one of those small, attractive stone-built towns with plenty of pubs and cafés and a good network of quiet lanes radiating out to the north and west. It is worth walking through the churchyard to Ruskin's View, painted by Turner. From the Market Square drop down to cross the River Lune via Devil's Bridge, shut to traffic since a new bridge was built in 1932. A steep climb through High Casterton and under the former Clapham to Sedbergh railway brings you up to the old Roman Road which ran south from the Lune Gorge to Ribchester, a Roman fort near Blackburn. This lane offers wonderful views west across the Lune valley and north towards the Howgill Fells. A long undulating section brings you to the start of the ride's main climb up through Barbondale. At times this has the feel of a Scottish glen, narrowing as you reach the summit where you are

rewarded with panoramic views over Dentdale. The descent is steep and twisty down to Gawthrop. You may wish to divert a mile to the east to visit the attractive village of Dent. The main route turns west on a tiny lane alongside the River Dee which is crossed at Rash Bridge, joining the 'main' road from Dent into the handsome town of Sedbergh, famous for its prestigious public school and gaining a reputation as

a centre for second-hand bookshops. From Sedbergh the route continues west to join a lovely quiet lane running down the west side of the Lune valley. Be prepared for one steep climb, coming as a surprise for what is otherwise a valley route. The woodlands are full of bluebells in late spring. The B6254 is joined at Kearstwick to take you back into Kirkby Lonsdale.

Overview
26 miles / 42 kilometres ● Moderate

Start
Market Square in Kirkby
Lonsdale, southeast of Kendal

Parking
Pay & Display car parks near
to Booths supermarket or free
parking near Devil's Bridge

Busy roads
The A684 exit from Sedbergh
is the busiest road on the ride
10 to **11**

Terrain
Long climb with some steep
sections and some flat bits
all the way from Devil's
Bridge at the start to the top
of Barbondale (820ft / 250m).
Undulating from Gawthrop
through Sedbergh back
to Kirkby Lonsdale with
one unexpected climb
(260ft / 80m) in the
Lune valley up to
Egholme Farm

Nearest railway
Oxenholme (Kendal)

Refreshments
Kirkby Lonsdale
Lots of choice

Dent (just off route)
Two cafés and two pubs

Sedbergh
Lots of choice

Other rides nearby
Ride 8
Page 50

Ride 11
Page 68

Ride 10

Ride 9
Page 56

Ride 12
Page 74

Map pages

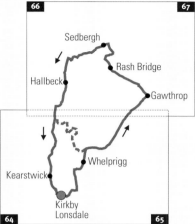

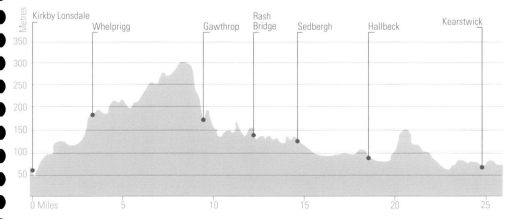

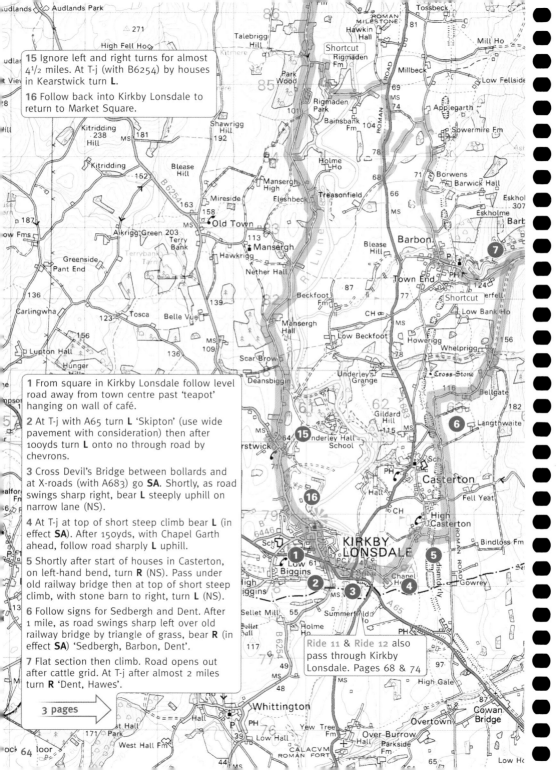

15 Ignore left and right turns for almost 4½ miles. At T-j (with B6254) by houses in Kearstwick turn **L**.

16 Follow back into Kirkby Lonsdale to return to Market Square.

1 From square in Kirkby Lonsdale follow level road away from town centre past 'teapot' hanging on wall of café.

2 At T-j with A65 turn **L** 'Skipton' (use wide pavement with consideration) then after 100yds turn **L** onto no through road by chevrons.

3 Cross Devil's Bridge between bollards and at X-roads (with A683) go **SA**. Shortly, as road swings sharp right, bear **L** steeply uphill on narrow lane (NS).

4 At T-j at top of short steep climb bear **L** (in effect **SA**). After 150yds, with Chapel Garth ahead, follow road sharply **L** uphill.

5 Shortly after start of houses in Casterton, on left-hand bend, turn **R** (NS). Pass under old railway bridge then at top of short steep climb, with stone barn to right, turn **L** (NS).

6 Follow signs for Sedbergh and Dent. After 1 mile, as road swings sharp left over old railway bridge by triangle of grass, bear **R** (in effect **SA**) 'Sedbergh, Barbon, Dent'.

7 Flat section then climb. Road opens out after cattle grid. At T-j after almost 2 miles turn **R** 'Dent, Hawes'.

Ride **11** & Ride **12** also pass through Kirkby Lonsdale. Pages 68 & 74

3 pages ➡

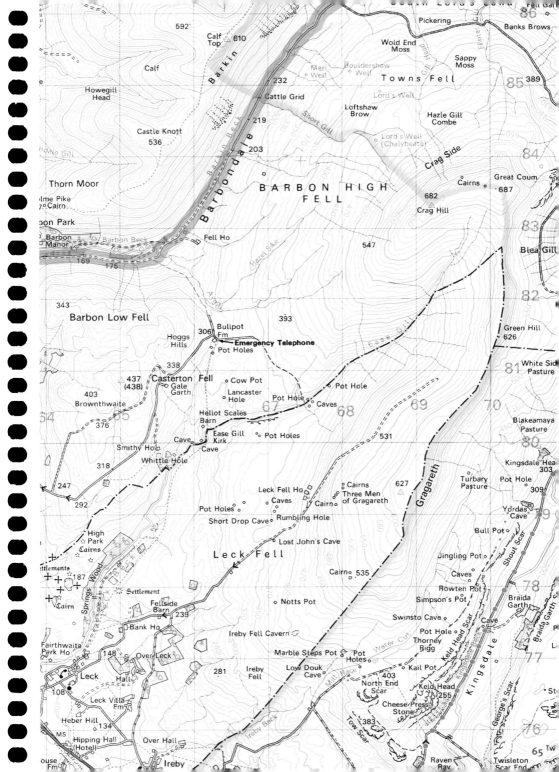

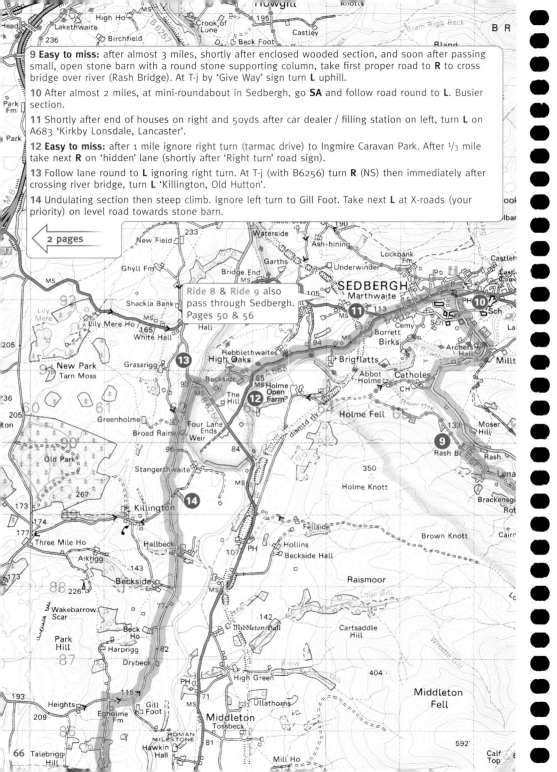

9 Easy to miss: after almost 3 miles, shortly after enclosed wooded section, and soon after passing small, open stone barn with a round stone supporting column, take first proper road to **R** to cross bridge over river (Rash Bridge). At T-j by 'Give Way' sign turn **L** uphill.

10 After almost 2 miles, at mini-roundabout in Sedbergh, go **SA** and follow road round to **L**. Busier section.

11 Shortly after end of houses on right and 50yds after car dealer / filling station on left, turn **L** on A683 'Kirkby Lonsdale, Lancaster'.

12 Easy to miss: after 1 mile ignore right turn (tarmac drive) to Ingmire Caravan Park. After 1/3 mile take next **R** on 'hidden' lane (shortly after 'Right turn' road sign).

13 Follow lane round to **L** ignoring right turn. At T-j (with B6256) turn **R** (NS) then immediately after crossing river bridge, turn **L** 'Killington, Old Hutton'.

14 Undulating section then steep climb. Ignore left turn to Gill Foot. Take next **L** at X-roads (your priority) on level road towards stone barn.

2 pages

Ride 8 & Ride 9 also pass through Sedbergh. Pages 50 & 56

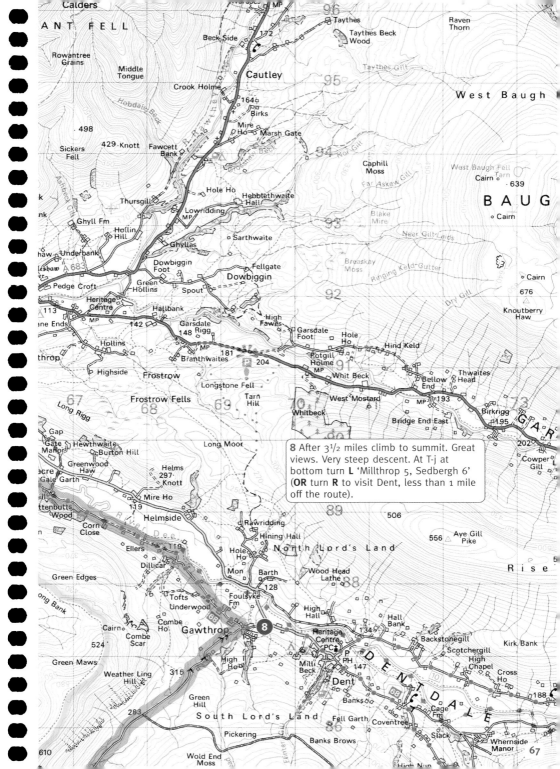

8 After 3½ miles climb to summit. Great views. Very steep descent. At T-j at bottom turn **L** 'Millthrop 5, Sedbergh 6' (**OR** turn **R** to visit Dent, less than 1 mile off the route).

Kirkby Lonsdale, Gatebeck & Killington

The previous ride explores the area north of Kirkby Lonsdale through Barbondale up to Sedbergh; this ride uses the network of lanes a little further west, criss-crossing the higher ground between the Lune valley in the east and the tributaries of the River Bela which joins the Kent estuary near Milnthorpe. For somewhere so close to Kendal and the M6 this area has a remote 'hidden' feel to it, but no less beautiful for

that. It lies between the two National Parks of the Lake District in the west and the Yorkshire Dales in the east. There is talk of extending both so they share a common boundary somewhere near the M6. The ride exits Kirkby Lonsdale to the northwest passing through a landscape of hedgerows, dry stone walls, lush pastures grazed by sheep and cattle, clumps of broadleaf woodland, stone farmhouses and verges full of wildflowers through spring

and summer. The views at the top of the first climb, beneath Warth Hill, looking west towards the Lakeland Fells are stunning. After descending steeply to cross the M6, a series of ever smaller valleys are followed north through Middleshaw, Ewebank and New Hutton. The busy A684 is crossed straight over onto a continuation of the quiet lane that contours around the base of Docker Fell and Lambrigg Fell. After recrossing the M6 the ride turns south, passing Killington Reservoir and joining what is known as the Old Scotch Road. This was an old drovers road as indicated by the dry stone walls set well back from the edge of the road, allowing the easy passage of flocks of sheep. The B6254 is joined near Old Town, and after a short climb you finish the ride with a fine long descent back to the charms of Kirkby Lonsdale.

Overview

28 miles / 45 kilometres ● Moderate

Start
St Mary's Church, Kirkby Lonsdale, southeast of Kendal

Parking
Pay & Display car parks near to Booths supermarket or free parking on the road used at the start of the ride, past the Orange Tree pub towards Old Town

Busy roads
Brief section on A684 near M6 with a tricky right turn **13**

Terrain
Long gentle climb (525ft / 160m) from the start to the highpoint below Warth Hill. The rest of the ride is undulating with several shorter climbs

Nearest railway
Oxenholme (Kendal)

Refreshments
Kirkby Lonsdale
Lots of choice

Oxenholme (2 miles off route)
Station Inn
T: 01539 724094

Other rides nearby

Ride 11

Ride 13
Page 80

Ride 10
Page 62

Ride 12
Page 74

Map pages

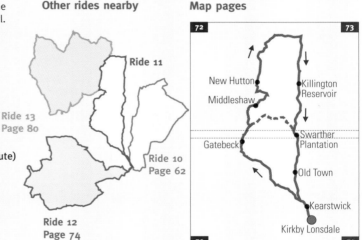

72 | 73
New Hutton
Middleshaw
Killington Reservoir
Gatebeck
Swarther Plantation
Old Town
Kearstwick
Kirkby Lonsdale
70 | 71

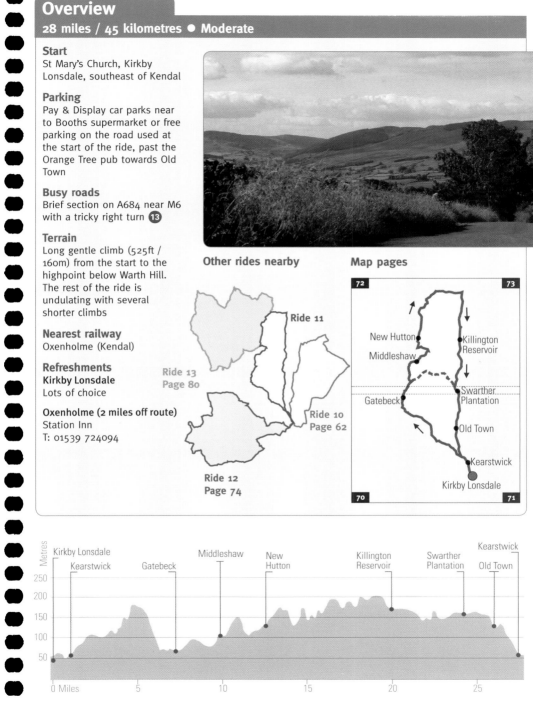

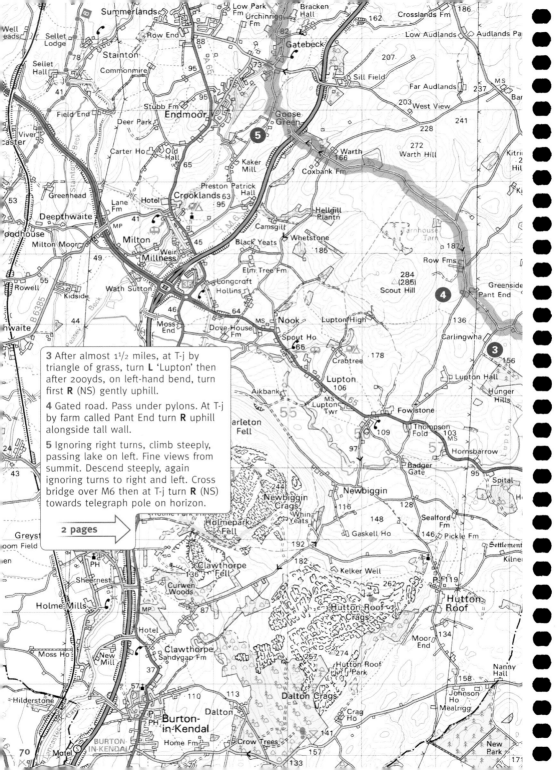

3 After almost 1¹⁄₂ miles, at T-j by triangle of grass, turn **L** 'Lupton' then after 200yds, on left-hand bend, turn first **R** (NS) gently uphill.

4 Gated road. Pass under pylons. At T-j by farm called Pant End turn **R** uphill alongside tall wall.

5 Ignoring right turns, climb steeply, passing lake on left. Fine views from summit. Descend steeply, again ignoring turns to right and left. Cross bridge over M6 then at T-j turn **R** (NS) towards telegraph pole on horizon.

2 pages ➡

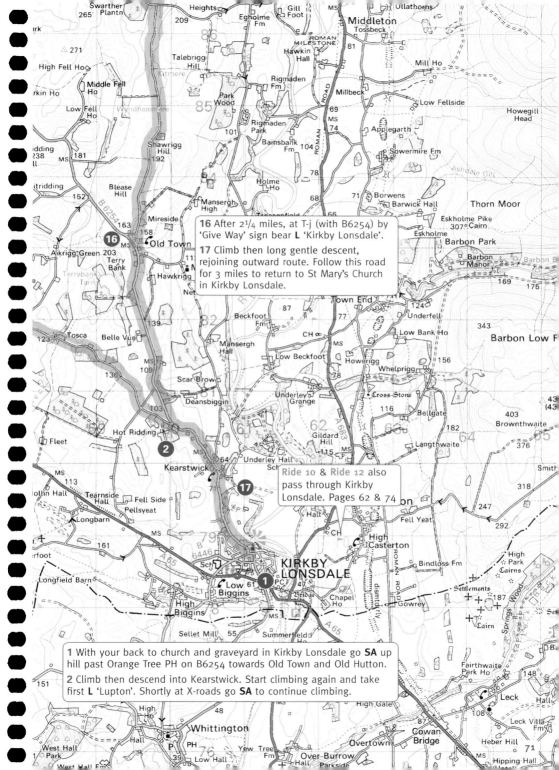

16 After 2¼ miles, at T-j (with B6254) by 'Give Way' sign bear **L** 'Kirkby Lonsdale'.

17 Climb then long gentle descent, rejoining outward route. Follow this road for 3 miles to return to St Mary's Church in Kirkby Lonsdale.

Ride **10** & Ride **12** also pass through Kirkby Lonsdale. Pages 62 & 74

1 With your back to church and graveyard in Kirkby Lonsdale go **SA** up hill past Orange Tree PH on B6254 towards Old Town and Old Hutton.

2 Climb then descend into Kearstwick. Start climbing again and take first **L** 'Lupton'. Shortly at X-roads go **SA** to continue climbing.

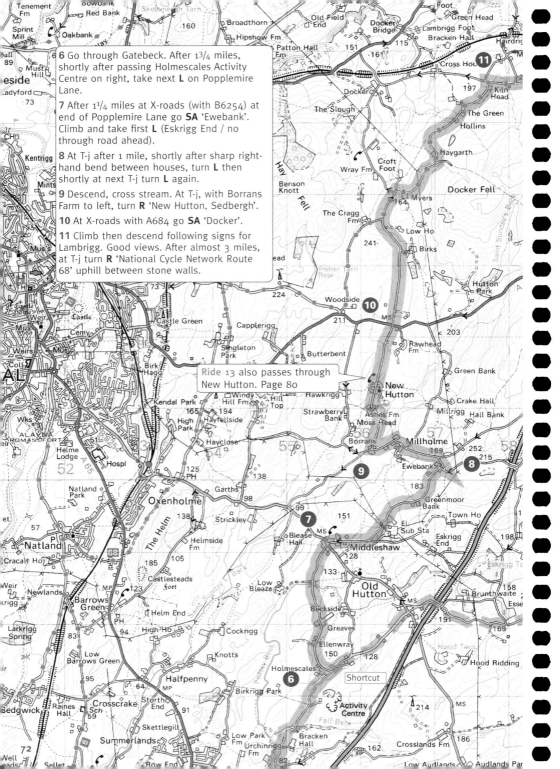

6 Go through Gatebeck. After 1¾ miles, shortly after passing Holmescales Activity Centre on right, take next **L** on Popplemire Lane.

7 After 1¼ miles at X-roads (with B6254) at end of Popplemire Lane go **SA** 'Ewebank'. Climb and take first **L** (Eskrigg End / no through road ahead).

8 At T-j after 1 mile, shortly after sharp right-hand bend between houses, turn **L** then shortly at next T-j turn **L** again.

9 Descend, cross stream. At T-j, with Borrans Farm to left, turn **R** 'New Hutton, Sedbergh'.

10 At X-roads with A684 go **SA** 'Docker'.

11 Climb then descend following signs for Lambrigg. Good views. After almost 3 miles, at T-j turn **R** 'National Cycle Network Route 68' uphill between stone walls.

Ride **13** also passes through New Hutton. Page 80

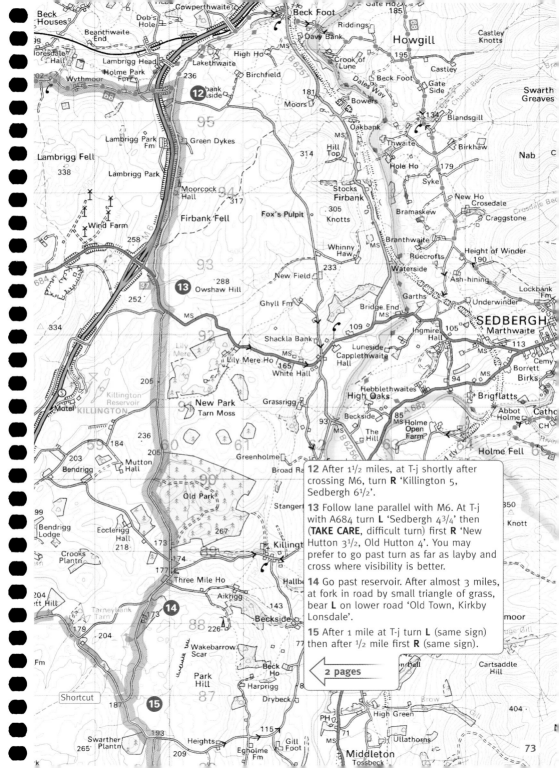

12 After 1½ miles, at T-j shortly after crossing M6, turn **R** 'Killington 5, Sedbergh 6½'.

13 Follow lane parallel with M6. At T-j with A684 turn **L** 'Sedbergh 4¾' then (**TAKE CARE**, difficult turn) first **R** 'New Hutton 3½, Old Hutton 4'. You may prefer to go past turn as far as layby and cross where visibility is better.

14 Go past reservoir. After almost 3 miles, at fork in road by small triangle of grass, bear **L** on lower road 'Old Town, Kirkby Lonsdale'.

15 After 1 mile at T-j turn **L** (same sign) then after ½ mile first **R** (same sign).

2 pages

Kirkby Lonsdale to Arnside

The third and final ride from Kirkby Lonsdale heads southwest to the coast at Silverdale and Arnside, with views over the expanse of Morecambe Bay towards the Lakeland Fells. Climb steadily from the square in Kirkby Lonsdale through Low and High Biggins to the sawmills at Hutton Roof. Look behind you for fine views of Ingleborough, one of Yorkshire's 'Three Peaks'. Descend then climb, soon running alongside what must be one of the quietest railway lines in the country, linking Carnforth to Settle. In quick succession the ride crosses the Lancaster Canal, the M6 motorway, the A6 and the West Coast Mainline. Climb steeply after Warton past the towering cliffs at Warton Crags (an old quarry). If you are interested in birds you may wish to divert slightly off the route to visit Leighton Moss, one of the few habitats of the Bittern. The roads are slightly busier through Silverdale and Arnside but this is a small price to pay for the magnificent views out across Morecambe Bay, at first to the southwest then, as you drop down into Arnside, to the northwest and the familiar outline of the central Lakeland Fells, as much a symbol of the Lake District as the Manhattan skyline is for New York. The busy coastal road north from Arnside is avoided in favour of an inland route via Storth which drops down through the beautifully landscaped parkland of Dallam Deer Park. Enjoy a couple of miles of the flattest roads in South Lakeland before joining the maze of lanes that link together and neatly avoid busy roads all the way back to Kirkby Lonsdale, passing right below the limestone bluff of Farleton Fell on a rollercoaster section to rejoin the outward route at High Biggins.

Overview
35 miles / 56 kilometres ● Moderate

Start
The Market Square, Kirkby
Lonsdale, southeast of Kendal

Parking
Pay & Display car parks near
to Booths supermarket or free
parking near Devil's Bridge

Busy roads
● Short section on the A6
then along Borwick Lane into
Warton **9** to **10**

● The roads near Silverdale
are busier **11** to **17**

Terrain
Several climbs of 150-300ft
(45-90m) but the highest point
of the ride is only 528ft (161m)

Nearest railway
Arnside

Refreshments
Kirkby Lonsdale
Lots of choice

Warton
George Washington PH
T: 01524 732865

South of Silverdale
Wolf House Gallery café
T: 01524 701405

Silverdale
Silverdale Hotel
T: 01524 701206
Royal Hotel
T: 01524 701266

Arnside
Lots of choice

Heversham
Blue Bell Hotel
T: 01539 562018

Farleton
Farleton View
Fishery Tea Room
T: 01539 567328

Other rides nearby

Ride 11
Page 68

Ride 12

Ride 10
Page 62

Map pages

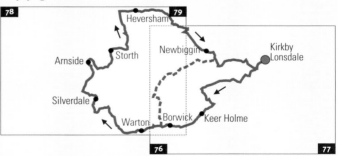

78 79
Heversham
Newbiggin
Kirkby
Lonsdale
Arnside Storth
Silverdale
Warton Borwick Keer Holme
76 77

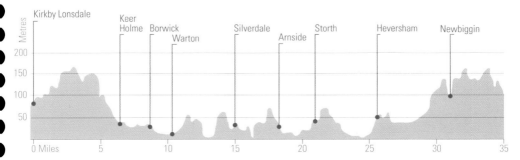

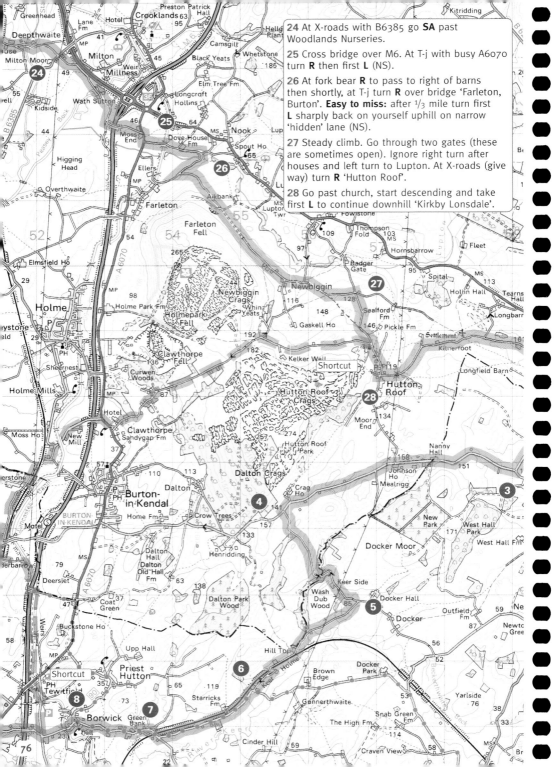

24 At X-roads with B6385 go **SA** past Woodlands Nurseries.

25 Cross bridge over M6. At T-j with busy A6070 turn **R** then first **L** (NS).

26 At fork bear **R** to pass to right of barns then shortly, at T-j turn **R** over bridge 'Farleton, Burton'. **Easy to miss:** after 1/3 mile turn first **L** sharply back on yourself uphill on narrow 'hidden' lane (NS).

27 Steady climb. Go through two gates (these are sometimes open). Ignore right turn after houses and left turn to Lupton. At X-roads (give way) turn **R** 'Hutton Roof'.

28 Go past church, start descending and take first **L** to continue downhill 'Kirkby Lonsdale'.

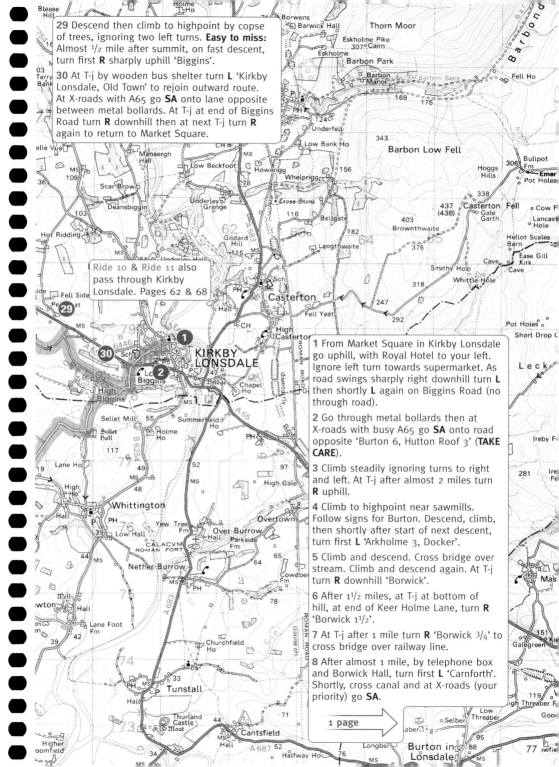

29 Descend then climb to highpoint by copse of trees, ignoring two left turns. **Easy to miss:** Almost 1/2 mile after summit, on fast descent, turn first **R** sharply uphill 'Biggins'.

30 At T-j by wooden bus shelter turn **L** 'Kirkby Lonsdale, Old Town' to rejoin outward route. At X-roads with A65 go **SA** onto lane opposite between metal bollards. At T-j at end of Biggins Road turn **R** downhill then at next T-j turn **R** again to return to Market Square.

Ride 10 & Ride 11 also pass through Kirkby Lonsdale. Pages 62 & 68

1 From Market Square in Kirkby Lonsdale go uphill, with Royal Hotel to your left. Ignore left turn towards supermarket. As road swings sharply right downhill turn **L** then shortly **L** again on Biggins Road (no through road).

2 Go through metal bollards then at X-roads with busy A65 go **SA** onto road opposite 'Burton 6, Hutton Roof 3' (**TAKE CARE**).

3 Climb steadily ignoring turns to right and left. At T-j after almost 2 miles turn **R** uphill.

4 Climb to highpoint near sawmills. Follow signs for Burton. Descend, climb, then shortly after start of next descent, turn first **L** 'Arkholme 3, Docker'.

5 Climb and descend. Cross bridge over stream. Climb and descend again. At T-j turn **R** downhill 'Borwick'.

6 After 1 1/2 miles, at T-j at bottom of hill, at end of Keer Holme Lane, turn **R** 'Borwick 1 1/2'.

7 At T-j after 1 mile turn **R** 'Borwick 3/4' to cross bridge over railway line.

8 After almost 1 mile, by telephone box and Borwick Hall, turn first **L** 'Carnforth'. Shortly, cross canal and at X-roads (your priority) go **SA**.

1 page →

9 Cross bridge over M6. At roundabout with A6 turn **L** then (**TAKE CARE**) first **R** onto Borwick Lane. Busier road.

10 At T-j with Main Street in Warton turn **L** 'Carnforth, Silverdale' then immediately before George Washington PH turn **R** uphill on Crag Road.

11 Long climb with steep section at start. Go past quarry. Long descent. After 2 miles, at T-j at end of Crag Road, bear **R** 'Silverdale 1³/4, Arnside 5'. Busier road.

12 Go over level crossing. At T-j by triangle of grass, turn **L** 'Silverdale 1'. Climb then after ¹/4 mile turn first **L** 'Jenny Brown's Point'.

13 Follow Lindeth Road round to right after Wolf House Gallery (Jenny Brown's Point is to the left).

14 At end of Lindeth Road turn **R** on Stankelt Road then shortly at T-j at top of climb turn **L** onto Emesgate Lane 'Arnside 3, Silverdale Centre'.

15 **Easy to miss:** on gentle descent about 300yds after church turn first **L** sharply back on yourself 'Arnside'.

16 After 2¹/4 miles climb to summit with good views of Morecambe Bay. Follow 'Promenade' signs down to shore and follow road to right by Albion PH.

17 Go past railway station, ignore left to Milnthorpe and Kendal. Cross level crossing, ignore first left on Carr Bank Road then shortly take next **L** on Storth Road 'Storth'.

18 After 1 mile, at X-roads in Storth (Give Way) turn **R** 'Beetham'.

19 At T-j after 1 mile turn **L** 'Haverbrack' then after ¹/4 mile of gentle descent first **R** 'National Cycle Network Route 6, Kendal 10'.

20 Tree-lined descent through parkland. At T-j (with B5282) turn **R** over bridge then **L** 'Cumbria Cycleway'.

21 After almost 1¹/2 miles follow road round sharp right-hand bend and ignore left turn. Go past Blue Bell Hotel and at X-roads with A6 go **SA** towards church.

22 Shortly, at T-j turn **R** then **L** onto Woodhouse Lane 'Wood House, Crooklands'.

23 Follow signs for Crooklands then Kirkby Lonsdale, ignoring right then left turn. At fork of lanes after 1¹/2 miles bear **L** 'Road narrows'.

24 At X-roads with B6385 go **SA** past Woodlands Nurseries.

25 Cross bridge over M6. At T-j with busy A6070 turn **R** then first **L** (NS).

26 At fork bear **R** to pass to right of barns then shortly, at T-j turn **R** over bridge 'Farleton, Burton'. **Easy to miss:** after ¹/3 mile turn first **L** sharply back on yourself uphill on narrow 'hidden' lane (NS).

← 2 pages

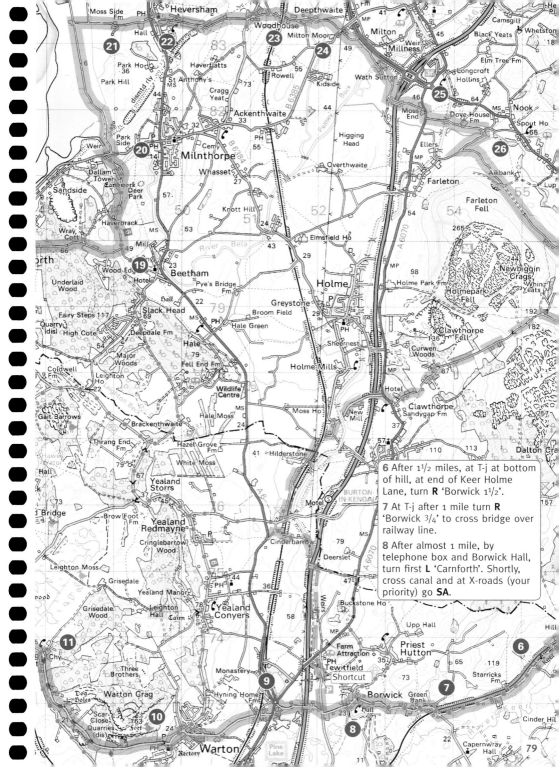

6 After 1½ miles, at T-j at bottom of hill, at end of Keer Holme Lane, turn **R** 'Borwick 1½'.

7 At T-j after 1 mile turn **R** 'Borwick ¾' to cross bridge over railway line.

8 After almost 1 mile, by telephone box and Borwick Hall, turn first **L** 'Carnforth'. Shortly, cross canal and at X-roads (your priority) go **SA**.

Ring around Kendal

I n many cases it is possible to create an enjoyable 'ring' ride around towns the size of Kendal by linking together lanes that cut across the main roads or 'spokes' that radiate out from the centre of the town. The busy roads are those that carry traffic into and out of the centre; the roads that run in concentric rings a few miles distant from the town are much quieter. Starting from Staveley, which has become a *de facto* cycling hub for South Cumbria, the ride heads east along the valley of the River Kent on a lovely wooded lane as far as Burneside before turning north up towards Longsleddale, a long dead-end valley formed by the River Sprint, leading towards Sadgill and Gatesgarth Pass. The A6 Shap Road is the first of the 'spokes' crossed on

this ride as you thread your way through the bewildering network of lanes that cross the River Mint, then the A685, then the West Coast Mainline as you follow the circle south through the hills high above Kendal. An indication of the remote feel of the landscape

through which the ride passes is that it is not until Barrows Green, on the A65 to the south of Kendal, that you come across the first pub since leaving Staveley. The rest of the ride is lower lying, lusher, more wooded with many more options for refreshments: there is a café at Sizergh Castle and pubs located every couple of miles, the Strickland Arms near Levens, and others in Brigsteer, Underbarrow and Crook. The views get better and better, first across the flat expanse of the Lyth Valley, then as you make the final climb towards the Lakeland Fells.

Overview

33 miles / 53 kilometres ● Moderate

Start
Mill Yard car park (Wheelbase),
Staveley, west of Kendal

Parking
As above

Busy roads
1/4 mile on A6 near
Watchgate **5**

Terrain
Several climbs of 150-300ft
(45-90m). Most of the ride lies
between 250-650ft (75-200m)
with a lower section parallel
with the Lyth Valley near
Brigsteer

Nearest railway
Oxenholme (Kendal)

Refreshments
Staveley
Lots of choice

Brigsteer
Wheatsheaf PH
T: 01539 568254

Underbarrow
Punchbowl PH
T: 01539 568234

Crook
Sun Inn
T: 01539 821351

Other rides nearby

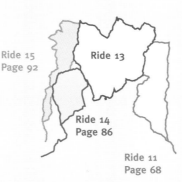

Ride 15
Page 92

Ride 13

Ride 14
Page 86

Ride 11
Page 68

Map pages

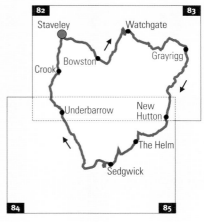

82   83
Staveley   Watchgate
Bowston   Grayrigg
Crook
Underbarrow   New Hutton
The Helm
Sedgwick
84   85

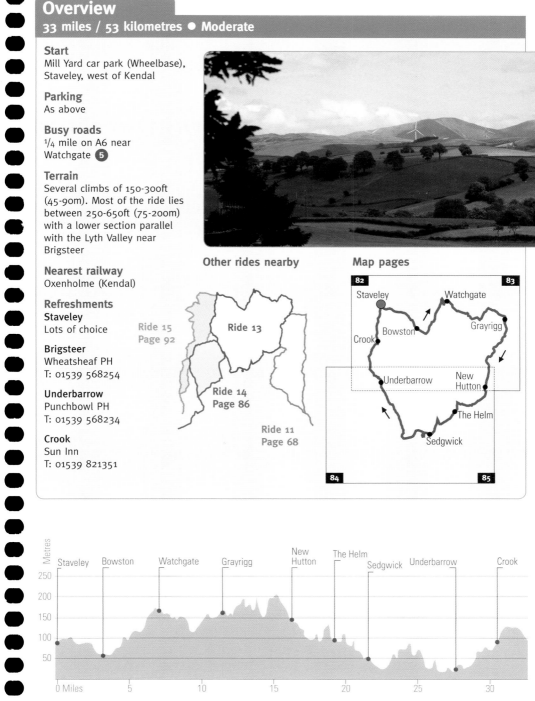

Metres

Staveley Bowston Watchgate Grayrigg New Hutton The Helm Sedgwick Underbarrow Crook

250
200
150
100
50

0 Miles   5   10   15   20   25   30

1 Exit Mill Yard car park in Staveley and turn sharp **R** 'No cars' sign in distance. At T-j at end of Back Lane turn **R** then after 250yds turn first **R** to cross river bridge 'Burneside'.

2 Over next 2½ miles, ignore three left turns - one immediately after bridge, one by low, square stone and cement platform and one in woodland by signs for 'Staveley' and 'Mirefoot'. Emerge from woodland, pass under power lines then on right-hand bend take next **L** by 'double' telegraph pole (NS).

3 At T-j, with 'Burneside' signposted to right, turn **L** then shortly **L** again 'Longsleddale'.

Ride 15 also passes through Staveley.
Page 92

20 Ignore turns to left and right for 2 miles. Keep following signs for Underbarrow and Crook. At T-j in Underbarrow turn **R** then **L** 'Crook' opposite Punchbowl PH.

21 After 2½ miles at T-j (with B5284 in Crook turn **R** uphill 'Kendal' on busier road. After 250yds turn first **L** 'Staveley 2' to continue climbing.

22 Short climb, long descent. At T-j in Staveley after 2 miles turn **R** 'Kendal (A591)'. After 300yds turn **L** into Mill Yard (Wheelbase) to return to the start.

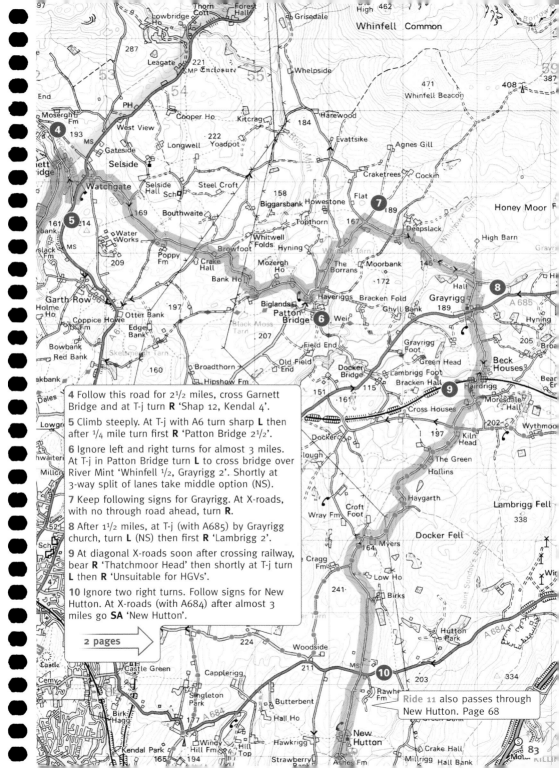

4 Follow this road for 2½ miles, cross Garnett Bridge and at T-j turn **R** 'Shap 12, Kendal 4'.

5 Climb steeply. At T-j with A6 turn sharp **L** then after ¼ mile turn first **R** 'Patton Bridge 2½'.

6 Ignore left and right turns for almost 3 miles. At T-j in Patton Bridge turn **L** to cross bridge over River Mint 'Whinfell ½, Grayrigg 2'. Shortly at 3-way split of lanes take middle option (NS).

7 Keep following signs for Grayrigg. At X-roads, with no through road ahead, turn **R**.

8 After 1½ miles, at T-j (with A685) by Grayrigg church, turn **L** (NS) then first **R** 'Lambrigg 2'.

9 At diagonal X-roads soon after crossing railway, bear **R** 'Thatchmoor Head' then shortly at T-j turn **L** then **R** 'Unsuitable for HGVs'.

10 Ignore two right turns. Follow signs for New Hutton. At X-roads (with A684) after almost 3 miles go **SA** 'New Hutton'.

2 pages ➡

Ride 11 also passes through New Hutton. Page 68

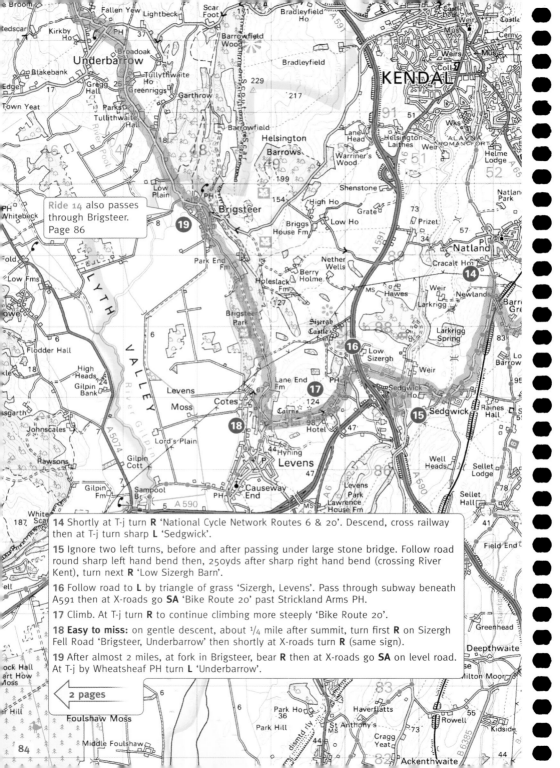

Ride 14 also passes through Brigsteer. Page 86

14 Shortly at T-j turn **R** 'National Cycle Network Routes 6 & 20'. Descend, cross railway then at T-j turn sharp **L** 'Sedgwick'.

15 Ignore two left turns, before and after passing under large stone bridge. Follow road round sharp left hand bend then, 250yds after sharp right hand bend (crossing River Kent), turn next **R** 'Low Sizergh Barn'.

16 Follow road to **L** by triangle of grass 'Sizergh, Levens'. Pass through subway beneath A591 then at X-roads go **SA** 'Bike Route 20' past Strickland Arms PH.

17 Climb. At T-j turn **R** to continue climbing more steeply 'Bike Route 20'.

18 **Easy to miss:** on gentle descent, about ¼ mile after summit, turn first **R** on Sizergh Fell Road 'Brigsteer, Underbarrow' then shortly at X-roads turn **R** (same sign).

19 After almost 2 miles, at fork in Brigsteer, bear **R** then at X-roads go **SA** on level road. At T-j by Wheatsheaf PH turn **L** 'Underbarrow'.

← 2 pages

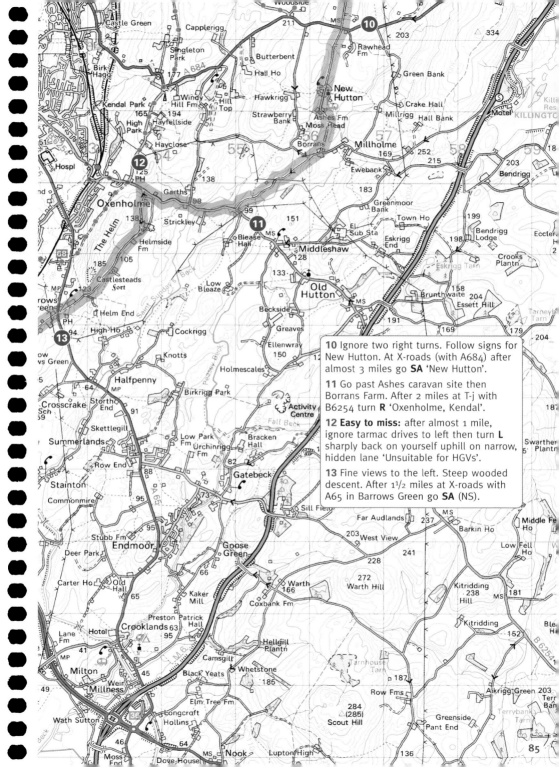

10 Ignore two right turns. Follow signs for New Hutton. At X-roads (with A684) after almost 3 miles go **SA** 'New Hutton'.

11 Go past Ashes caravan site then Borrans Farm. After 2 miles at T-j with B6254 turn **R** 'Oxenholme, Kendal'.

12 **Easy to miss:** after almost 1 mile, ignore tarmac drives to left then turn **L** sharply back on yourself uphill on narrow, hidden lane 'Unsuitable for HGVs'.

13 Fine views to the left. Steep wooded descent. After 1½ miles at X-roads with A65 in Barrows Green go **SA** (NS).

Grange & the Lyth Valley

This is by far the easiest ride in the book - the southern section from Grange Golf Club via Meathop, Gilpin Bridge and the Lyth Valley to Brigsteer would even be suitable for families with younger children as it is almost all flat and the roads carry very little traffic. The A590 is crossed safely via an underpass and there is even an ice cream factory at Holme Farm (near Grange) that could be the goal to aim for, should you start from near Levens. Unfortunately there is no parking at the golf club so the ride starts from Grange

railway station car park and uses a ¹/₂-mile section of the busy B5277 before turning off across Meathop Marsh. This is rich arable country, something of an oddity in this part of Cumbria where most of the land is pasture for sheep and cattle. Go past a tall rock outcrop and into woodland through Meathop

(a gentle climb). After passing under the A590 you turn east on what was the old road before the dual carriageway was built. This old road is now reduced in parts to just one lane so carries very little traffic. A traffic-free link at Gilpin Bridge neatly avoids the A590 and gives access to the wonderful flat lane heading north up the Lyth Valley to Brigsteer. Gird your loins for a few climbs over the next few miles as you follow the head of the Lyth Valley through Underbarrow and Crosthwaite, crossing the A5074 before the steepest hill of the day, climbing to a dizzying 210ft (64m) beneath Whitbarrow Scar. A lovely undulating lane through woodland leads back to Witherslack where the outward route is rejoined through Meathop to Grange.

Overview
26 miles / 41 kilometres ● Easy

Start
Grange-over-Sands railway
station

Parking
As above

Busy roads
The B5277 from Grange railway
station to the turn off to the
golf club is busy ❶

Terrain
The easiest ride in the book,
never climbing above 210ft
(64m). Much of the first part of
the ride is pancake flat

Nearest railway
Grange-over-Sands

Refreshments
Grange
Lots of choice

East of Grange
Holme Farm Ice Cream Factory
(shut Mondays and Tuesdays)
T: 01539 532991

Witherslack
Derby Arms PH
T: 01539 552207

Gilpin Bridge
Gilpin Bridge Inn
T: 01539 522206

Brigsteer
Wheatsheaf PH
T: 01539 568254

Crosthwaite
Punchbowl PH
T: 01539 568237

Other rides nearby
Ride 15
Page 92

Ride 13
Page 80

Ride 14

Ride 12
Page 74

Map pages

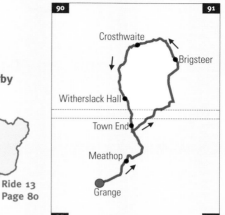

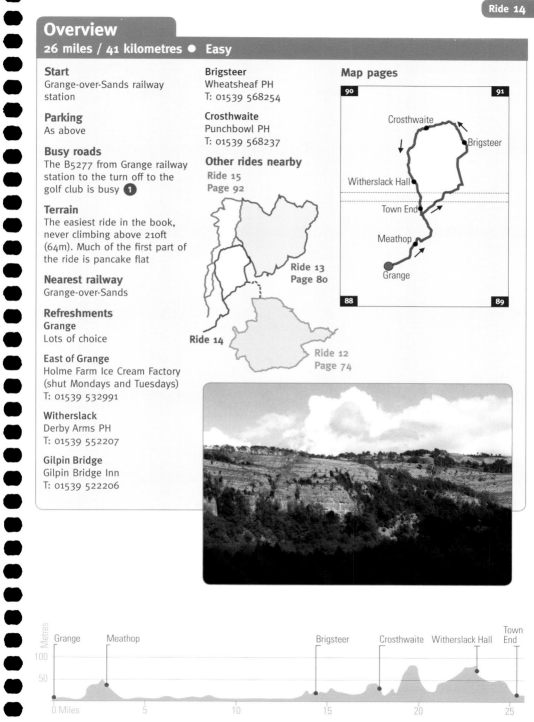

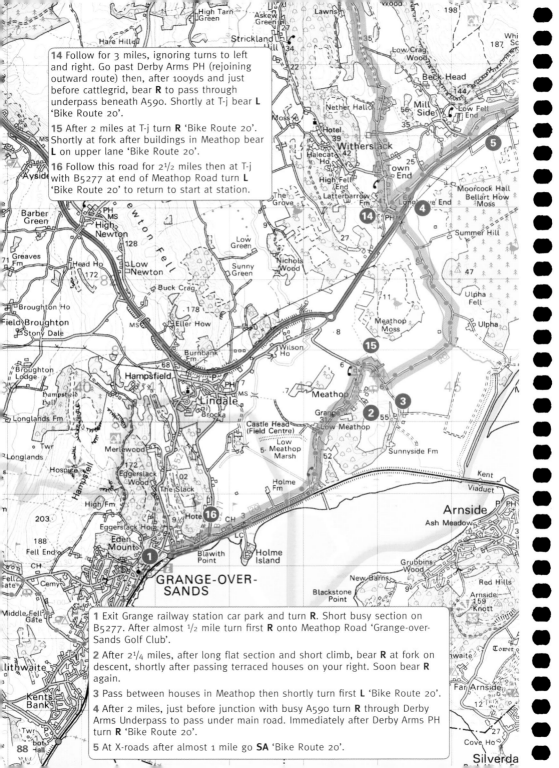

14 Follow for 3 miles, ignoring turns to left and right. Go past Derby Arms PH (rejoining outward route) then, after 100yds and just before cattlegrid, bear **R** to pass through underpass beneath A590. Shortly at T-j bear **L** 'Bike Route 20'.

15 After 2 miles at T-j turn **R** 'Bike Route 20'. Shortly at fork after buildings in Meathop bear **L** on upper lane 'Bike Route 20'.

16 Follow this road for 2½ miles then at T-j with B5277 at end of Meathop Road turn **L** 'Bike Route 20' to return to start at station.

1 Exit Grange railway station car park and turn **R**. Short busy section on B5277. After almost ½ mile turn first **R** onto Meathop Road 'Grange-over-Sands Golf Club'.

2 After 2¼ miles, after long flat section and short climb, bear **R** at fork on descent, shortly after passing terraced houses on your right. Soon bear **R** again.

3 Pass between houses in Meathop then shortly turn first **L** 'Bike Route 20'.

4 After 2 miles, just before junction with busy A590 turn **R** through Derby Arms Underpass to pass under main road. Immediately after Derby Arms PH turn **R** 'Bike Route 20'.

5 At X-roads after almost 1 mile go **SA** 'Bike Route 20'.

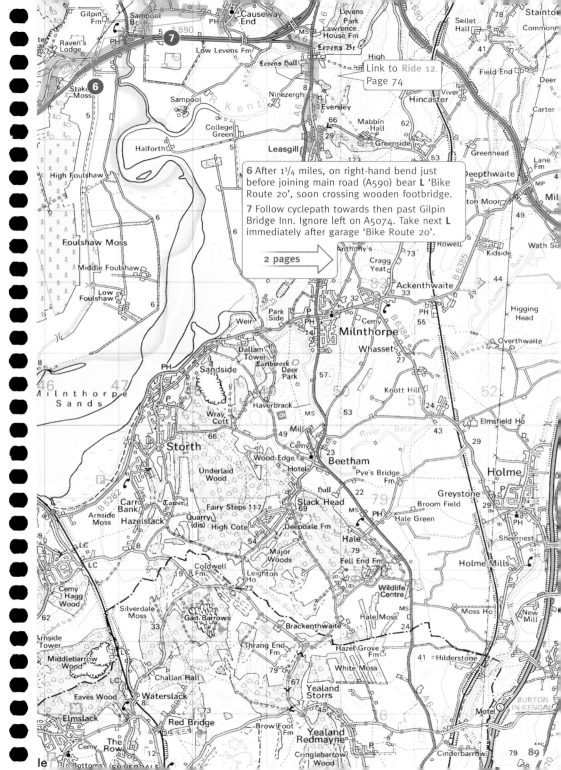

Link to Ride 12. Page 74

6 After 1¼ miles, on right-hand bend just before joining main road (A590) bear **L** 'Bike Route 20', soon crossing wooden footbridge.

7 Follow cyclepath towards then past Gilpin Bridge Inn. Ignore left on A5074. Take next **L** immediately after garage 'Bike Route 20'.

2 pages ➡

11 Ups and downs for 1 mile. Shortly after 'Crosthwaite' village sign, with church ahead, turn **L** 'Lyth' then immediately **R★** 'Unsuitable for HGVs'.

OR go SA for pub in Crosthwaite

12 At X-roads (with A5074) go **SA** 'Cartmel'.

13 Steep climb. Descend, ignoring right turn to Bowland Bridge. Climb past cluster of buildings at Pool Bank Farm and shortly follow road sharply round to **L**, ignoring right turn downhill on bend.

2 pages

Ride 15 overlaps along this stretch. Page 92

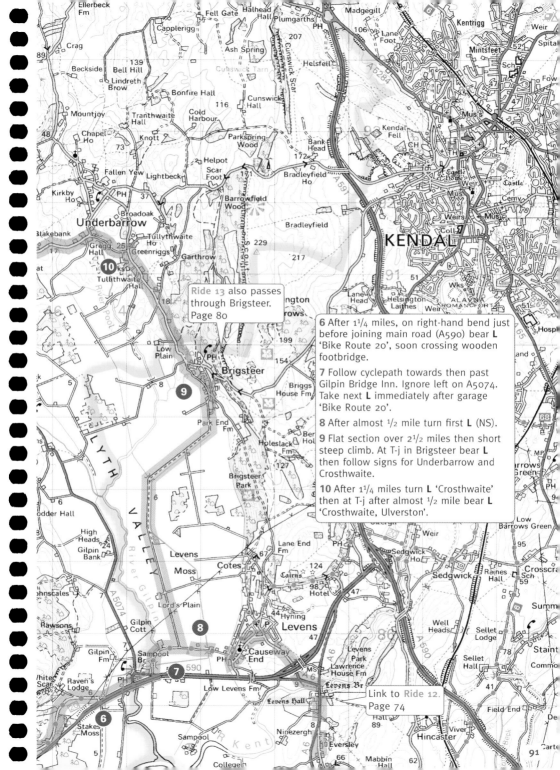

Ride 13 also passes through Brigsteer. Page 80

6 After 1¼ miles, on right-hand bend just before joining main road (A590) bear **L** 'Bike Route 20', soon crossing wooden footbridge.

7 Follow cyclepath towards then past Gilpin Bridge Inn. Ignore left on A5074. Take next **L** immediately after garage 'Bike Route 20'.

8 After almost ½ mile turn first **L** (NS).

9 Flat section over 2½ miles then short steep climb. At T-j in Brigsteer bear **L** then follow signs for Underbarrow and Crosthwaite.

10 After 1¼ miles turn **L** 'Crosthwaite' then at T-j after almost ½ mile bear **L** 'Crosthwaite, Ulverston'.

Link to Ride 12. Page 74

91

Lindale to Staveley

This ride is located entirely within the Lake District National Park and yet you will be astonished at how quiet the lanes are linking the villages of Lindale and Staveley. The ride starts by sneaking out of Lindale on the wonderfully named Back o' the Fell Road. The Winster valley provides ideal conditions for cycling – it is relatively flat, very quiet and yet the views all around are stunning with a mixture of woodland, pasture, attractive old stone-built farmhouses, rocky outcrops and distant fells. This is definitely a ride that improves as you do it a second and third time as there are quite a few junctions linking the lanes that keep you away from the busier roads. At the north end of the Winster valley the terrain gets hillier, climbing to a highpoint on the outward leg just to the north of Crook. There are splendid views north towards the hills above Kentmere and east over the Kent Valley towards the Howgills. Staveley has become Cumbria's best cycling hub with an excellent bike shop and café, and a plethora of road and off-road routes starting from the large car park at Mill Yard. There is also a top-grade vergeside cyclepath linking Staveley to Windermere, running parallel to the A591. This is followed as far as Ings where the pub, the Watermill Inn, boasts an enormous range of real ale. The longest climb of the day takes you up through gate after gate on what feels like a hidden, forgotten network of lanes with ever better views in all directions. A short downhill section on the busy B5284 (Crook Road) will snap you out of your reverie before you plunge back into the labyrinth of lanes leading south through Crosthwaite to rejoin the upper end of the Winster valley and a gentle return to Lindale.

Overview

31 miles / 50 kilometres ● Moderate

Start
Lindale Inn, Lindale, near
Grange-over-Sands

Parking
On-street parking up the hill
past the shop

Busy roads
1 mile on B5284 east of
Bowness **15** to **16**

Terrain
The southern half of the ride
is fairly flat. Several more hills
towards Staveley. The longest
climb (295ft / 90m) is south
from Ings to Borwick Fold

Nearest railway
Staveley

Other rides nearby

Refreshments
Lindale
Lindale Inn
T: 01539 532416

Crosthwaite
Punchbowl PH
T: 01539 568237

Crook
Sun Inn
T: 01539 821351

Staveley
Lots of choice

Ings
Watermill Inn
T: 01539 821309

Bowland Bridge
(just off route)
Hare & Hounds Country Inn
T: 01539 568333

Map pages

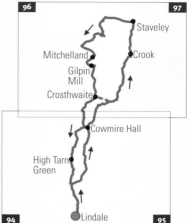

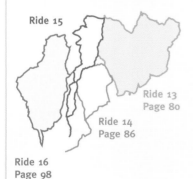

Ride 15

Ride 13
Page 80

Ride 14
Page 86

Ride 16
Page 98

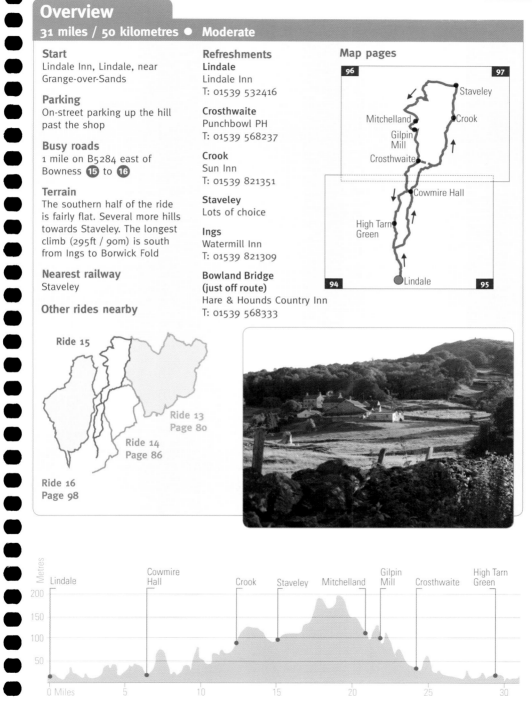

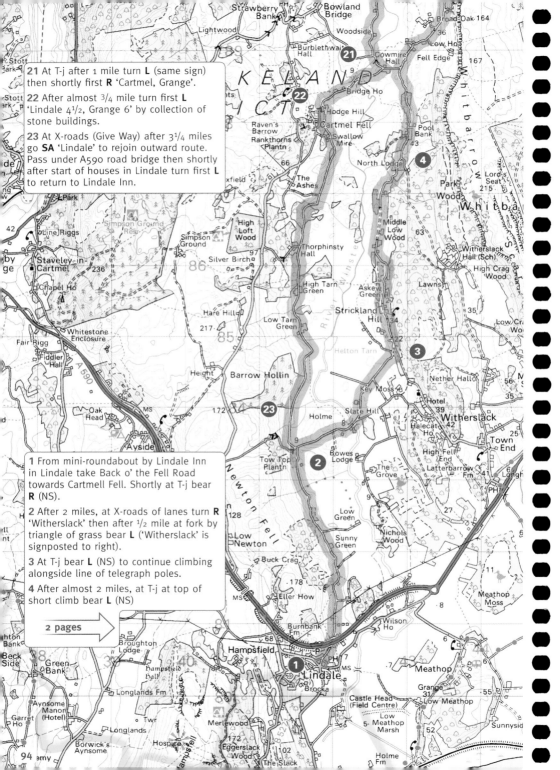

21 At T-j after 1 mile turn **L** (same sign) then shortly first **R** 'Cartmel, Grange'.

22 After almost ³/₄ mile turn first **L** 'Lindale 4¹/₂, Grange 6' by collection of stone buildings.

23 At X-roads (Give Way) after 3¹/₄ miles go **SA** 'Lindale' to rejoin outward route. Pass under A590 road bridge then shortly after start of houses in Lindale turn first **L** to return to Lindale Inn.

1 From mini-roundabout by Lindale Inn in Lindale take Back o' the Fell Road towards Cartmell Fell. Shortly at T-j bear **R** (NS).

2 After 2 miles, at X-roads of lanes turn **R** 'Witherslack' then after ¹/₂ mile at fork by triangle of grass bear **L** ('Witherslack' is signposted to right).

3 At T-j bear **L** (NS) to continue climbing alongside line of telegraph poles.

4 After almost 2 miles, at T-j at top of short climb bear **L** (NS)

2 pages ➡

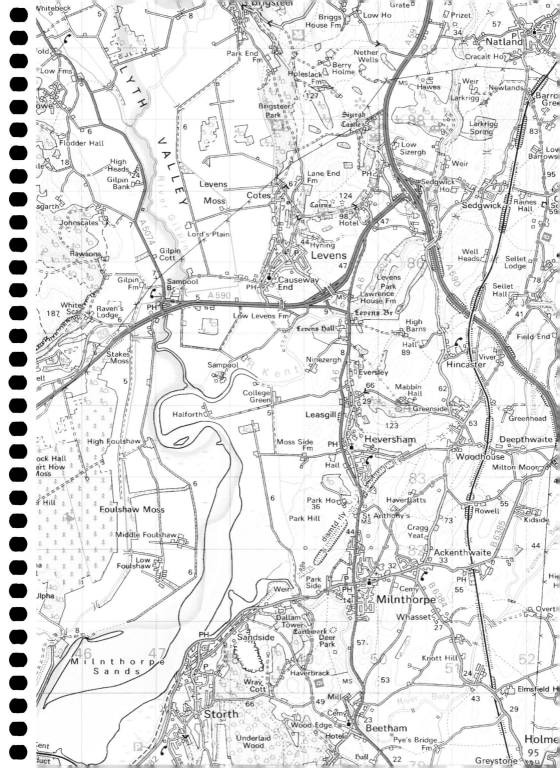

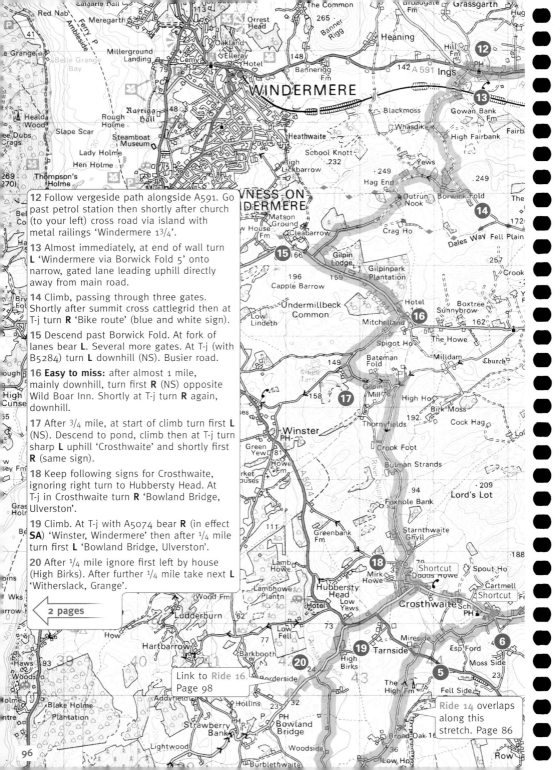

12 Follow vergeside path alongside A591. Go past petrol station then shortly after church (to your left) cross road via island with metal railings 'Windermere 1¾'.

13 Almost immediately, at end of wall turn **L** 'Windermere via Borwick Fold 5' onto narrow, gated lane leading uphill directly away from main road.

14 Climb, passing through three gates. Shortly after summit cross cattlegrid then at T-j turn **R** 'Bike route' (blue and white sign).

15 Descend past Borwick Fold. At fork of lanes bear **L**. Several more gates. At T-j (with B5284) turn **L** downhill (NS). Busier road.

16 **Easy to miss:** after almost 1 mile, mainly downhill, turn first **R** (NS) opposite Wild Boar Inn. Shortly at T-j turn **R** again, downhill.

17 After ¾ mile, at start of climb turn first **L** (NS). Descend to pond, climb then at T-j turn sharp **L** uphill 'Crosthwaite' and shortly first **R** (same sign).

18 Keep following signs for Crosthwaite, ignoring right turn to Hubbersty Head. At T-j in Crosthwaite turn **R** 'Bowland Bridge, Ulverston'.

19 Climb. At T-j with A5074 bear **R** (in effect **SA**) 'Winster, Windermere' then after ¼ mile turn first **L** 'Bowland Bridge, Ulverston'.

20 After ¼ mile ignore first left by house (High Birks). After further ¼ mile take next **L** 'Witherslack, Grange'.

2 pages

Link to Ride 16. Page 98

Ride 14 overlaps along this stretch. Page 86

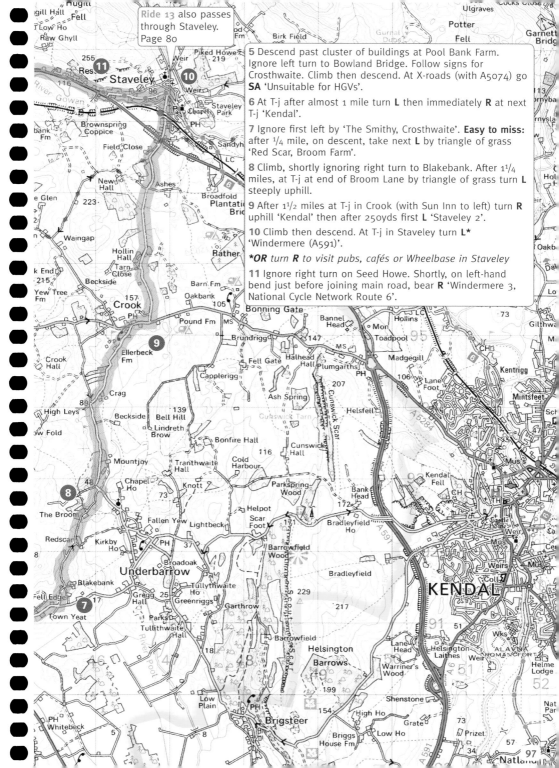

Ride 13 also passes through Staveley. Page 80

5 Descend past cluster of buildings at Pool Bank Farm. Ignore left turn to Bowland Bridge. Follow signs for Crosthwaite. Climb then descend. At X-roads (with A5074) go **SA** 'Unsuitable for HGVs'.

6 At T-j after almost 1 mile turn **L** then immediately **R** at next T-j 'Kendal'.

7 Ignore first left by 'The Smithy, Crosthwaite'. **Easy to miss:** after 1/4 mile, on descent, take next **L** by triangle of grass 'Red Scar, Broom Farm'.

8 Climb, shortly ignoring right turn to Blakebank. After 1 1/4 miles, at T-j at end of Broom Lane by triangle of grass turn **L** steeply uphill.

9 After 1 1/2 miles at T-j in Crook (with Sun Inn to left) turn **R** uphill 'Kendal' then after 250yds first **L** 'Staveley 2'.

10 Climb then descend. At T-j in Staveley turn **L*** 'Windermere (A591)'.

***OR** turn **R** to visit pubs, cafés or Wheelbase in Staveley*

11 Ignore right turn on Seed Howe. Shortly, on left-hand bend just before joining main road, bear **R** 'Windermere 3, National Cycle Network Route 6'.

Backbarrow, Cartmel & the ferry across Windermere

The ferry across Windermere is one of Cumbria's cycling highlights: as you approach from east or west on your bike you glide past the queues of cars to arrive right at the front and the views from the crossing are simply magnificent. The second half of the ride explores the land either side of Windermere, England's longest lake. Starting from Backbarrow, which is located on the River Leven at the southern end of the lake, the first part of the ride climbs south over the hills to visit the delightful village of Cartmel. This has become a foodie paradise with several good restaurants,

pubs, cafés and delicatessens and is home to the famous Cartmel Sticky Toffee Pudding. The Priory was founded in 1188 and has superb stained-glass windows and choir stalls carved with strange creatures. The 14th-century gatehouse near the square was once part of the Priory. Two or three times a year the village is thronged with thousands of people attending Cartmel Races. Obviously the roads will be busier on these weekends (see www.cartmel-racecourse.co.uk for dates). After visiting Cartmel, head north, climbing steadily through Field Broughton and High Newton to the highpoint of the ride (565ft / 172m),

high above the Winster valley with views to the limestone bulk of Whitbarrow Scar. Drop down to Bowland Bridge and continue north through Winster on the secret network of lanes to bring you to a short busy downhill section of the Crook Road (B5284) leading directly to the ferry. On the west side of the lake the ride passes through some beautiful broadleaf woodland then climbs over the Furness Fells into the Rusland Valley where you may well see deer grazing. A final woodland climb over Hill Top drops you back to the start at Backbarrow.

Overview

28 miles / 45 kilometres ● Moderate / Strenuous

Start
Small free car park just north of Whitewater Hotel in Backbarrow, off the A590 at the south end of Lake Windermere

Parking
From Newby Bridge and the A590 follow signs for Lakeland Motor Museum. About 100yds after the museum, opposite the start of the houses on the right, bear left uphill into a small car park by recycling facilities

Busy roads
● B5284 to the east of the ferry (downhill) **17** to **18**

● All the roads around Cartmel will be busier on race days (2-3 times a year - see www. cartmel-racecourse.co.uk) **4** to **6**

Terrain
There is a steep climb from the start (460ft / 140m) past Bigland Hall and a second more gentle climb over several miles from Cartmel to Newton Fell (also 460ft / 140m). After Low Cunsey there is a 395ft (120m) climb with a steep section near to Graythwaite Hall. Several shorter climbs

Nearest railway
Cark & Cartmel

Refreshments
Backbarrow
Whitewater Hotel
T: 01539 531133

Cartmel
Lots of choice

High Newton
Crown PH
T: 01539 530613

Bowland Bridge
Hare & Hounds Country Inn
T: 01539 568333

Winster
Brown Horse PH
T: 01539 443443

Far Sawrey (just off route)
Sawrey Hotel
T: 01539 443425

Other rides nearby

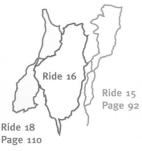

Ride 16

Ride 15
Page 92

Ride 18
Page 110

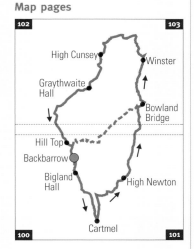

Map pages

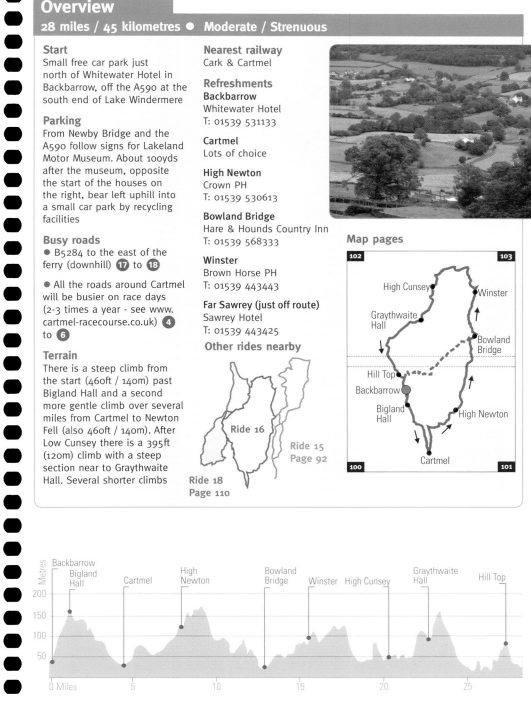

High Cunsey
Winster
Graythwaite Hall
Bowland Bridge
Hill Top
Backbarrow
Bigland Hall
High Newton
Cartmel

102 103 100 101

Metres

Backbarrow
Bigland Hall
Cartmel
High Newton
Bowland Bridge
Winster High Cunsey
Graythwaite Hall
Hill Top

200
150
100
50

0 Miles   5   10   15   20   25

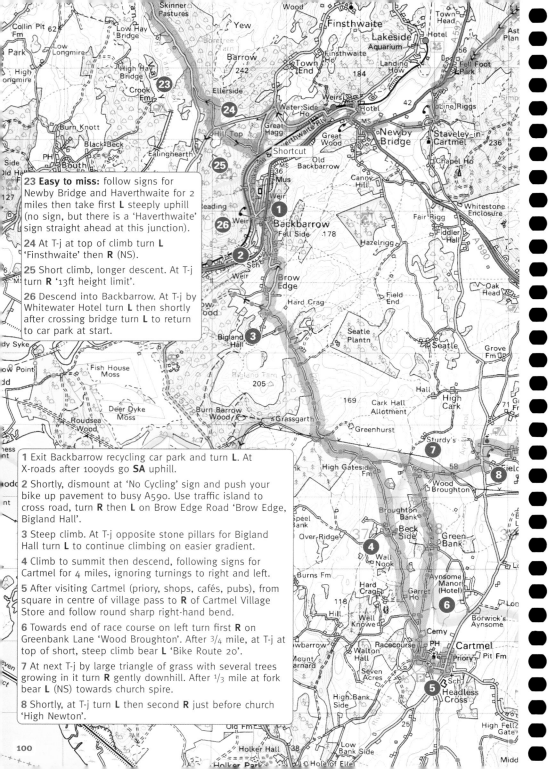

23 Easy to miss: follow signs for Newby Bridge and Haverthwaite for 2 miles then take first **L** steeply uphill (no sign, but there is a 'Haverthwaite' sign straight ahead at this junction).

24 At T-j at top of climb turn **L** 'Finsthwaite' then **R** (NS).

25 Short climb, longer descent. At T-j turn **R** '13ft height limit'.

26 Descend into Backbarrow. At T-j by Whitewater Hotel turn **L** then shortly after crossing bridge turn **L** to return to car park at start.

1 Exit Backbarrow recycling car park and turn **L**. At X-roads after 100yds go **SA** uphill.

2 Shortly, dismount at 'No Cycling' sign and push your bike up pavement to busy A590. Use traffic island to cross road, turn **R** then **L** on Brow Edge Road 'Brow Edge, Bigland Hall'.

3 Steep climb. At T-j opposite stone pillars for Bigland Hall turn **L** to continue climbing on easier gradient.

4 Climb to summit then descend, following signs for Cartmel for 4 miles, ignoring turnings to right and left.

5 After visiting Cartmel (priory, shops, cafés, pubs), from square in centre of village pass to **R** of Cartmel Village Store and follow round sharp right-hand bend.

6 Towards end of race course on left turn first **R** on Greenbank Lane 'Wood Broughton'. After 3/4 mile, at T-j at top of short, steep climb bear **L** 'Bike Route 20'.

7 At next T-j by large triangle of grass with several trees growing in it turn **R** gently downhill. After 1/3 mile at fork bear **L** (NS) towards church spire.

8 Shortly, at T-j turn **L** then second **R** just before church 'High Newton'.

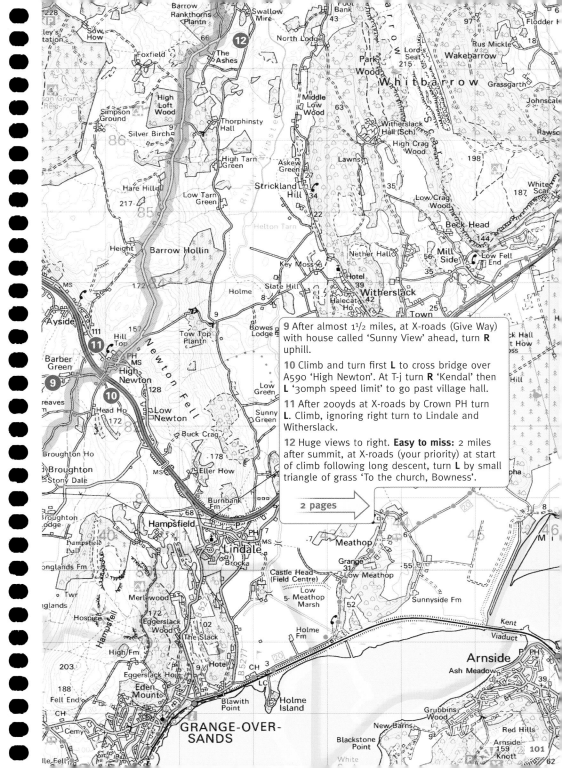

9 After almost 1½ miles, at X-roads (Give Way) with house called 'Sunny View' ahead, turn **R** uphill.

10 Climb and turn first **L** to cross bridge over A590 'High Newton'. At T-j turn **R** 'Kendal' then **L** '30mph speed limit' to go past village hall.

11 After 200yds at X-roads by Crown PH turn **L**. Climb, ignoring right turn to Lindale and Witherslack.

12 Huge views to right. **Easy to miss:** 2 miles after summit, at X-roads (your priority) at start of climb following long descent, turn **L** by small triangle of grass 'To the church, Bowness'.

2 pages →

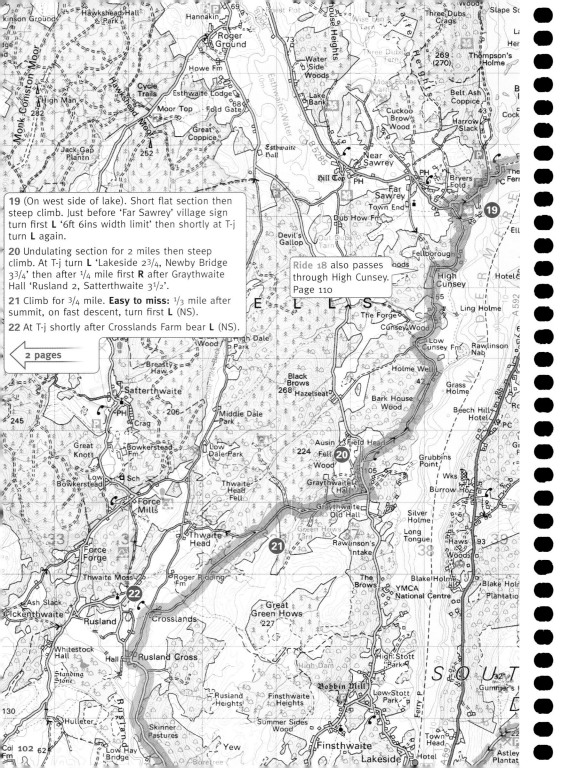

19 (On west side of lake). Short flat section then steep climb. Just before 'Far Sawrey' village sign turn first **L** '6ft 6ins width limit' then shortly at T-j turn **L** again.

20 Undulating section for 2 miles then steep climb. At T-j turn **L** 'Lakeside 2³/₄, Newby Bridge 3³/₄' then after ¹/₄ mile first **R** after Graythwaite Hall 'Rusland 2, Satterthwaite 3¹/₂'.

21 Climb for ³/₄ mile. **Easy to miss:** ¹/₃ mile after summit, on fast descent, turn first **L** (NS).

22 At T-j shortly after Crosslands Farm bear **L** (NS).

Ride **18** also passes through High Cunsey. Page 110

2 pages

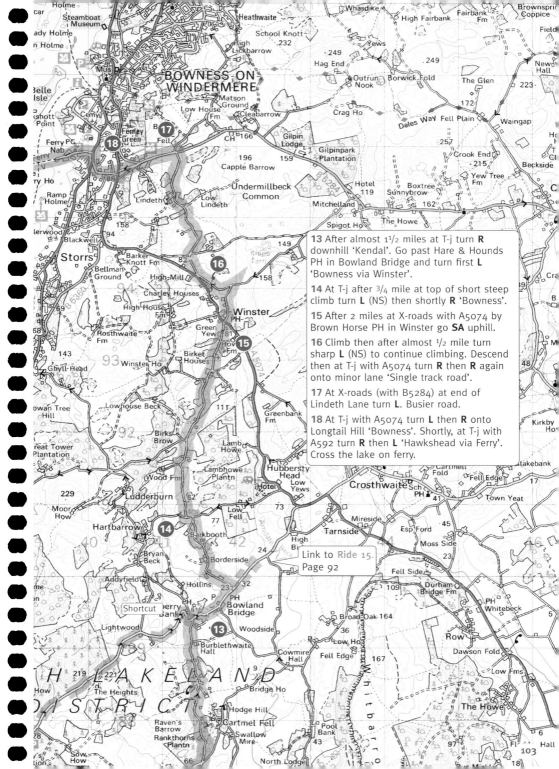

13 After almost 1½ miles at T-j turn **R** downhill 'Kendal'. Go past Hare & Hounds PH in Bowland Bridge and turn first **L** 'Bowness via Winster'.

14 At T-j after ¾ mile at top of short steep climb turn **L** (NS) then shortly **R** 'Bowness'.

15 After 2 miles at X-roads with A5074 by Brown Horse PH in Winster go **SA** uphill.

16 Climb then after almost ½ mile turn sharp **L** (NS) to continue climbing. Descend then at T-j with A5074 turn **R** then **R** again onto minor lane 'Single track road'.

17 At X-roads (with B5284) at end of Lindeth Lane turn **L**. Busier road.

18 At T-j with A5074 turn **L** then **R** onto Longtail Hill 'Bowness'. Shortly, at T-j with A592 turn **R** then **L** 'Hawkshead via Ferry'. Cross the lake on ferry.

Link to **Ride 15**. Page 92

Shortcut

Grasmere, Hawkshead & Coniston

If the Lake District National Park lies at the heart of Cumbria then this ride lies right at the heart of the National Park - you cannot get more central than Grasmere, Elterwater and Skelwith Bridge and the views are stupendous on every mile of the ride. A mixture of lanes and short sections of stone tracks that form part of the National Cycle Network enable you against all odds to avoid the busy roads of the Central Lakes. After a short flat section south from the start in Grasmere, a very steep climb above the lake (Grasmere) up and over Red Bank drops you steeply down to Skelwith

Bridge, crossing the River Brathay, the main river taking water from the central fells into Lake Windermere. After a brief glimpse of a busy road (the A593) the ride plunges back into the secret realm of narrow walled lanes climbing through Skelwith Fold to the famous Drunken Duck Inn at Barngates. This is more of a restaurant than a pub but the tables outside command some of the finest lakeland views of any pub. Wiggle your way east then south through High Wray to Hawkshead, a village thriving on its outdoor clothes shops. The next stop is Coniston but as the main connecting road (the B5285) is busy and steep, the ride diverts off this to Knipe Fold, rejoining it at High Cross, at the top of the hill, giving a long fine descent to Coniston. A good stone track through woodland north from Coniston leads to the start of the dead-end road climbing

through beautiful scenery up to the deep and atmospheric quarry lake at Hodge Close. There are parts of the next mile where you may prefer to walk as there are two short rocky sections. Emerge close to the Three Shires Inn, located a couple of miles east of the old meeting point of the three counties of Westmorland, Cumberland and Lancashire. You may wish to extend the ride by turning west to explore the Langdales. The ride described here descends to Colwith, turns north to Elterwater then climbs steeply to rejoin the outward route and return to Grasmere.

NB There are two off-road stretches on good quality stone tracks between Coniston and Little Langdale. These sections are passable on road bikes but it would help to fit tyres of 28mm or wider.

Overview

25 miles / 40 kilometres ● Strenuous

Start
Lamb Inn, Grasmere

Parking
Several car parks

Busy roads
Four short busy sections, none more than ½ mile:
● A593 at Skelwith Bridge **4**

● B5286 east of Drunken Duck Inn **7**

● B5285 north from Hawkshead **10**

● B5285 at High Cross, west of Hawkshead (downhill) **12**

Terrain
Several short steep climbs of 150-300ft (45-90m) and two longer ones:
● From Hawkshead to the top of Hawkshead Hill (425ft / 130m)

● From Coniston to High Tilberthwaite (490ft / 150m)

Nearest railway
Windermere

Refreshments
Grasmere
Lots of choice

Skelwith Bridge
Chesters Café
T: 01539 434711

Barngates
(south of Skelwith Bridge)
Drunken Duck Inn
T: 01539 436347

Hawkshead
Lots of choice

Coniston
Lots of choice

Little Langdale
Three Shires Inn
T: 01539 437215

Elterwater
Britannia Inn
T: 01539 437210

Other rides nearby

Ride 17

Ride 19
Page 116

Ride 18
Page 110

Map pages

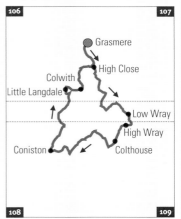

106 | 107
Grasmere
High Close
Colwith
Little Langdale
Low Wray
High Wray
Coniston
Colthouse
108 | 109

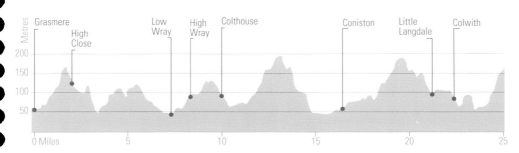

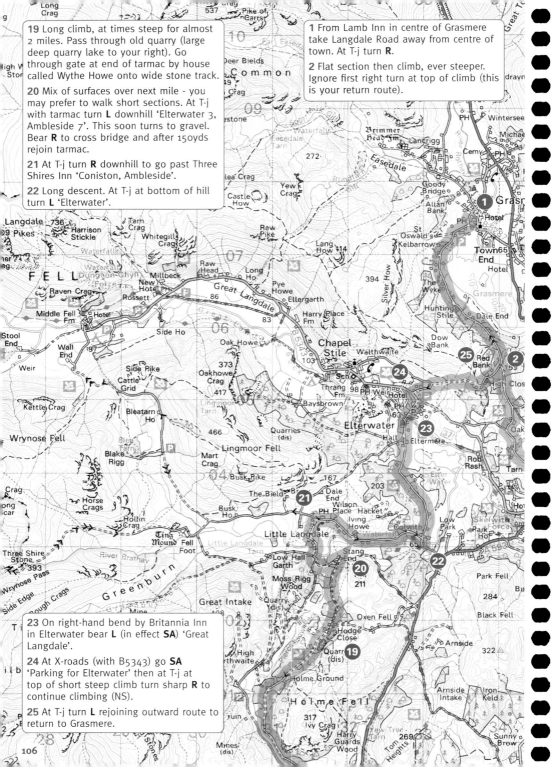

19 Long climb, at times steep for almost 2 miles. Pass through old quarry (large deep quarry lake to your right). Go through gate at end of tarmac by house called Wythe Howe onto wide stone track.

20 Mix of surfaces over next mile - you may prefer to walk short sections. At T-j with tarmac turn **L** downhill 'Elterwater 3, Ambleside 7'. This soon turns to gravel. Bear **R** to cross bridge and after 150yds rejoin tarmac.

21 At T-j turn **R** downhill to go past Three Shires Inn 'Coniston, Ambleside'.

22 Long descent. At T-j at bottom of hill turn **L** 'Elterwater'.

1 From Lamb Inn in centre of Grasmere take Langdale Road away from centre of town. At T-j turn **R**.

2 Flat section then climb, ever steeper. Ignore first right turn at top of climb (this is your return route).

23 On right-hand bend by Britannia Inn in Elterwater bear **L** (in effect **SA**) 'Great Langdale'.

24 At X-roads (with B5343) go **SA** 'Parking for Elterwater' then at T-j at top of short steep climb turn sharp **R** to continue climbing (NS).

25 At T-j turn **L** rejoining outward route to return to Grasmere.

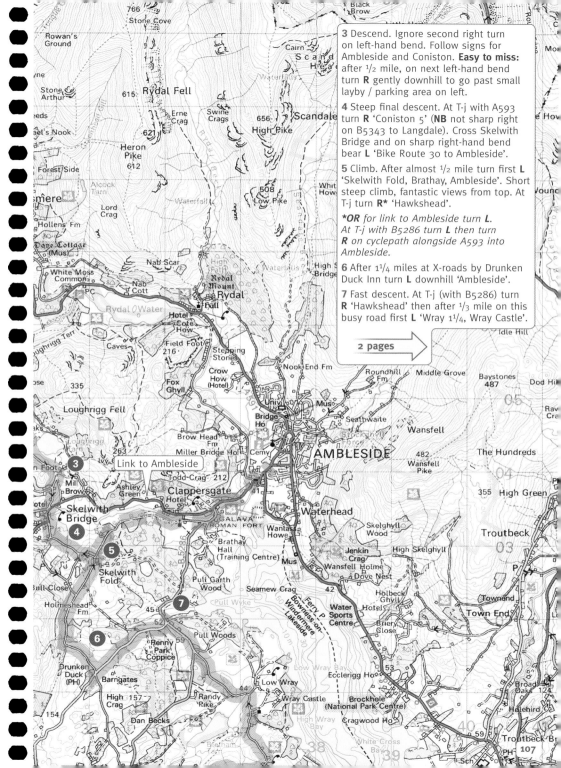

3 Descend. Ignore second right turn on left-hand bend. Follow signs for Ambleside and Coniston. **Easy to miss:** after 1/2 mile, on next left-hand bend turn **R** gently downhill to go past small layby / parking area on left.

4 Steep final descent. At T-j with A593 turn **R** 'Coniston 5' (**NB** not sharp right on B5343 to Langdale). Cross Skelwith Bridge and on sharp right-hand bend bear **L** 'Bike Route 30 to Ambleside'.

5 Climb. After almost 1/2 mile turn first **L** 'Skelwith Fold, Brathay, Ambleside'. Short steep climb, fantastic views from top. At T-j turn **R*** 'Hawkshead'.

*OR *for link to Ambleside turn* **L**. *At T-j with B5286 turn* **L** *then turn* **R** *on cyclepath alongside A593 into Ambleside.*

6 After 1 1/4 miles at X-roads by Drunken Duck Inn turn **L** downhill 'Ambleside'.

7 Fast descent. At T-j (with B5286) turn **R** 'Hawkshead' then after 1/3 mile on this busy road first **L** 'Wray 1 1/4, Wray Castle'.

2 pages ⟶

Link to Ambleside

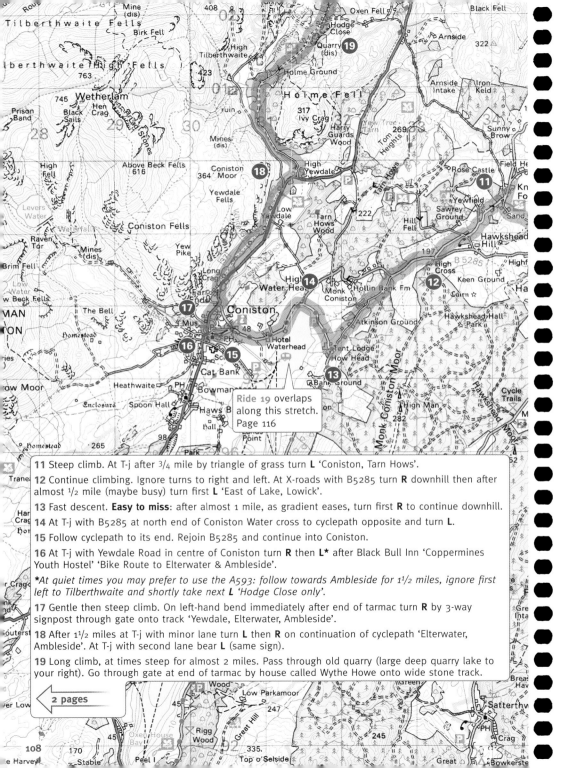

11 Steep climb. At T-j after 3/4 mile by triangle of grass turn **L** 'Coniston, Tarn Hows'.

12 Continue climbing. Ignore turns to right and left. At X-roads with B5285 turn **R** downhill then after almost 1/2 mile (maybe busy) turn first **L** 'East of Lake, Lowick'.

13 Fast descent. **Easy to miss**: after almost 1 mile, as gradient eases, turn first **R** to continue downhill.

14 At T-j with B5285 at north end of Coniston Water cross to cyclepath opposite and turn **L**.

15 Follow cyclepath to its end. Rejoin B5285 and continue into Coniston.

16 At T-j with Yewdale Road in centre of Coniston turn **R** then **L*** after Black Bull Inn 'Coppermines Youth Hostel' 'Bike Route to Elterwater & Ambleside'.

***At quiet times you may prefer to use the A593: follow towards Ambleside for 1 1/2 miles, ignore first left to Tilberthwaite and shortly take next **L** 'Hodge Close only'.*

17 Gentle then steep climb. On left-hand bend immediately after end of tarmac turn **R** by 3-way signpost through gate onto track 'Yewdale, Elterwater, Ambleside'.

18 After 1 1/2 miles at T-j with minor lane turn **L** then **R** on continuation of cyclepath 'Elterwater, Ambleside'. At T-j with second lane bear **L** (same sign).

19 Long climb, at times steep for almost 2 miles. Pass through old quarry (large deep quarry lake to your right). Go through gate at end of tarmac by house called Wythe Howe onto wide stone track.

Ride 19 overlaps along this stretch. Page 116

2 pages

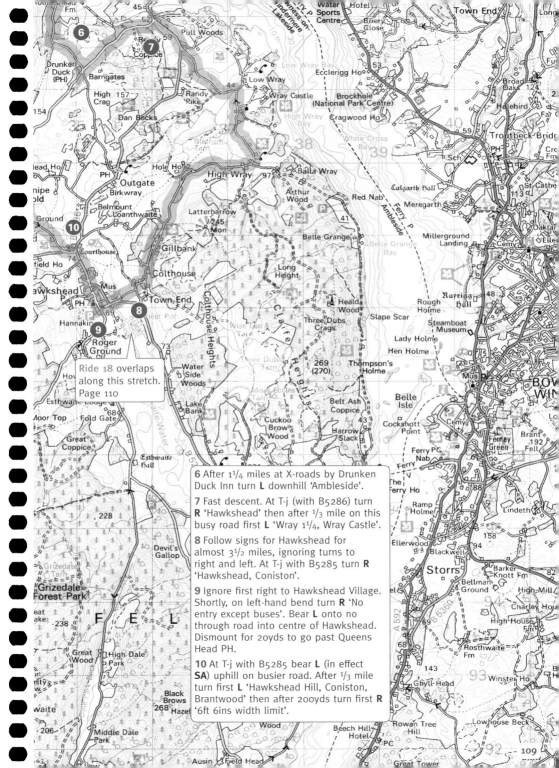

6 After 1¹/₄ miles at X-roads by Drunken Duck Inn turn **L** downhill 'Ambleside'.

7 Fast descent. At T-j (with B5286) turn **R** 'Hawkshead' then after ¹/₃ mile on this busy road first **L** 'Wray 1¹/₄, Wray Castle'.

8 Follow signs for Hawkshead for almost 3¹/₂ miles, ignoring turns to right and left. At T-j with B5285 turn **R** 'Hawkshead, Coniston'.

9 Ignore first right to Hawkshead Village. Shortly, on left-hand bend turn **R** 'No entry except buses'. Bear **L** onto no through road into centre of Hawkshead. Dismount for 20yds to go past Queens Head PH.

10 At T-j with B5285 bear **L** (in effect **SA**) uphill on busier road. After ¹/₃ mile turn first **L** 'Hawkshead Hill, Coniston, Brantwood' then after 200yds turn first **R** '6ft 6ins width limit'.

Ride 18 overlaps along this stretch. Page 110

Haverthwaite to Hawkshead

The area lying between Coniston Water and Windermere has the feel of an island about it: the two lakes and the rivers that feed into them then drain from them into Morecambe Bay enclose the land from Skelwith Bridge south to Newby Bridge and Penny Bridge. The previous ride explores the land at the north of the 'island'; this figure-of-eight ride uses the lanes that cross the area from Hawkshead in the north to Haverthwaite in the south. Starting from Haverthwaite the ride crosses the River Leven (connecting Windermere to the coast) and follows an off-road track through woodland to Greenodd,

using an underpass to avoid the busy A590. Turn north from Penny Bridge, soon entering a world of isolated farmhouses, outcrops of rocks, lush pasture and broadleaf woodland. If you just want a short ride, turn south at Rusland down

the Rusland Valley back to Haverthwaite. For the full ride, climb northeast through mixed woodland past Graythwaite Hall then drop down to the shores of Windermere through Low and High Cunsey. Hill Top at Near Sawrey was bought by Beatrix Potter in 1905 and it was here that she wrote many of her famous stories. A short section of busier road, mainly downhill past Esthwaite Water, brings you to Hawkshead and a wide choice of refreshments. Turn south along the opposite shores of Esthwaite Water, before long leaving the main road heading for Lakeside and branching off onto a quieter lane climbing steeply to the ride's highpoint at 560ft (170m) before a long gentle descent first alongside Dale Park Beck then Rusland Pool to return to Haverthwaite.

Overview

26 miles / 42 kilometres ● Moderate

Start
The Sports & Community Hall at the south end of Haverthwaite by a green signboard at Grid Reference SD 342837. Haverthwaite is just off the A590 between Newby Bridge and Ulverston

Parking
As above

Busy roads
About 2½ miles on the B5285 northwest of Far Sawrey ⑬ to ⑭

Terrain
The northern half of the ride is hillier than the southern half: there is a 460ft (140m) climb from the Rusland Valley east to Graythwaite Hall and 310ft (95m) climb south from Hawkshead towards High Dale Park

Nearest railway
Cark & Cartmel Station

Refreshments
Greenodd
Ship Inn
T: 01229 861304

Oxen Park
Manor House PH
T: 01229 861345

Far Sawrey
Sawrey Hotel
T: 01539 443425

Near Sawrey
Tower Bank Arms PH
T: 01539 436334

Hawkshead
Lots of choice

**Booth
(just off the route)**
White Hart Inn
T: 01229 861229

Other rides nearby

Ride 17
Page 104

Ride 16
Page 98

Ride 19
Page 116

Ride 18

Map pages

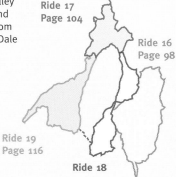

114
115
Hawkshead
Far Sawrey
Graythwaite Hall
Rusland
Rusland Cross
Colton
Ealinghearth
Penny Bridge
Haverthwaite
112
113

Metres

Haverthwaite | Penny Bridge | Colton | Rusland | Graythwaite Hall | Far Sawrey | Hawkshead | Rusland Cross | Ealinghearth

200
150
100
50

0 Miles   5   10   15   20   25

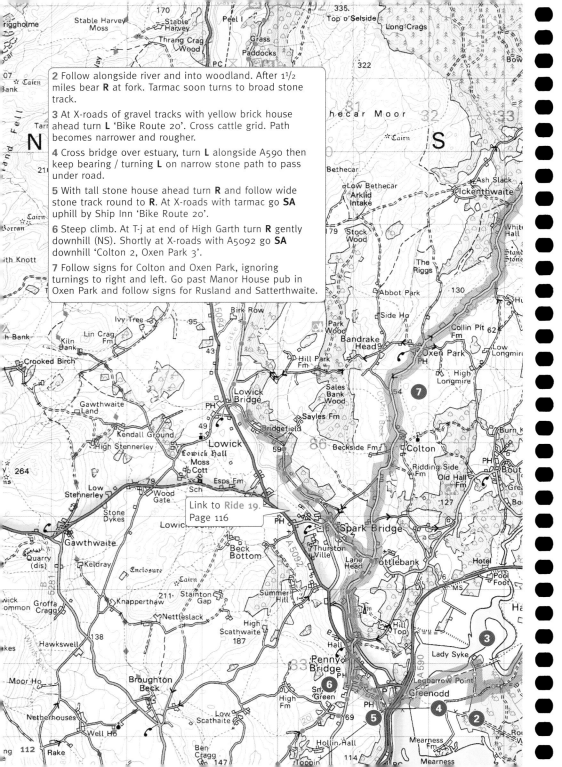

2 Follow alongside river and into woodland. After 1½ miles bear **R** at fork. Tarmac soon turns to broad stone track.

3 At X-roads of gravel tracks with yellow brick house ahead turn **L** 'Bike Route 20'. Cross cattle grid. Path becomes narrower and rougher.

4 Cross bridge over estuary, turn **L** alongside A590 then keep bearing / turning **L** on narrow stone path to pass under road.

5 With tall stone house ahead turn **R** and follow wide stone track round to **R**. At X-roads with tarmac go **SA** uphill by Ship Inn 'Bike Route 20'.

6 Steep climb. At T-j at end of High Garth turn **R** gently downhill (NS). Shortly at X-roads with A5092 go **SA** downhill 'Colton 2, Oxen Park 3'.

7 Follow signs for Colton and Oxen Park, ignoring turnings to right and left. Go past Manor House pub in Oxen Park and follow signs for Rusland and Satterthwaite.

Link to **Ride 19.**
Page 116

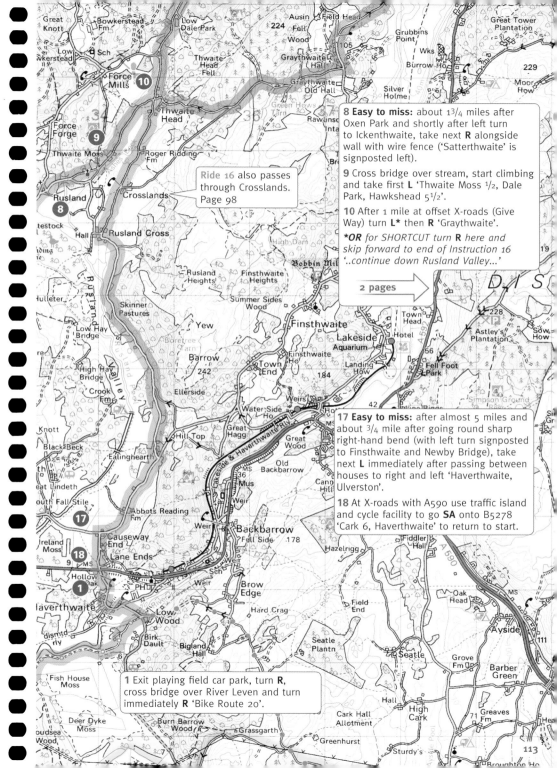

8 Easy to miss: about 1¾ miles after Oxen Park and shortly after left turn to Ickenthwaite, take next **R** alongside wall with wire fence ('Satterthwaite' is signposted left).

9 Cross bridge over stream, start climbing and take first **L** 'Thwaite Moss ½, Dale Park, Hawkshead 5½'.

10 After 1 mile at offset X-roads (Give Way) turn **L*** then **R** 'Graythwaite'.

***OR** for SHORTCUT turn **R** here and skip forward to end of Instruction 16 '..continue down Rusland Valley...'*

Ride 16 also passes through Crosslands. Page 98

2 pages ➡

17 Easy to miss: after almost 5 miles and about ¾ mile after going round sharp right-hand bend (with left turn signposted to Finsthwaite and Newby Bridge), take next **L** immediately after passing between houses to right and left 'Haverthwaite, Ulverston'.

18 At X-roads with A590 use traffic island and cycle facility to go **SA** onto B5278 'Cark 6, Haverthwaite' to return to start.

1 Exit playing field car park, turn **R**, cross bridge over River Leven and turn immediately **R** 'Bike Route 20'.

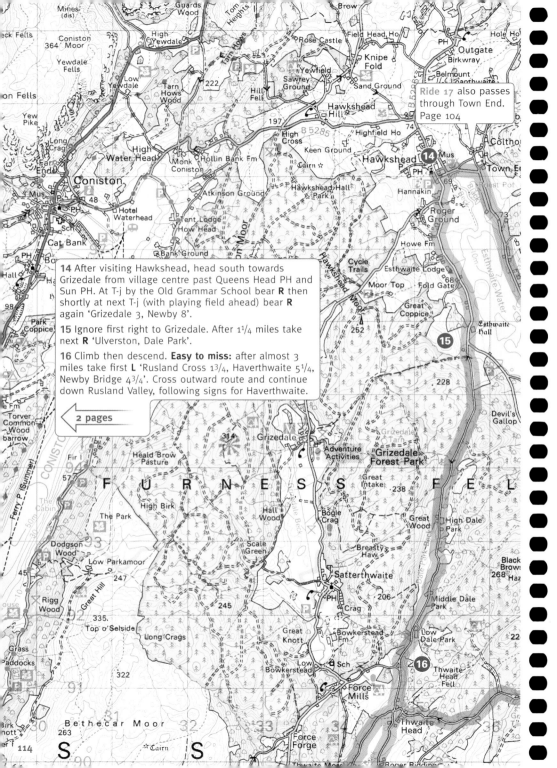

Ride 17 also passes through Town End. Page 104

14 After visiting Hawkshead, head south towards Grizedale from village centre past Queens Head PH and Sun PH. At T-j by the Old Grammar School bear **R** then shortly at next T-j (with playing field ahead) bear **R** again 'Grizedale 3, Newby 8'.

15 Ignore first right to Grizedale. After 1¼ miles take next **R** 'Ulverston, Dale Park'.

16 Climb then descend. **Easy to miss:** after almost 3 miles take first **L** 'Rusland Cross 1¾, Haverthwaite 5¼, Newby Bridge 4¾'. Cross outward route and continue down Rusland Valley, following signs for Haverthwaite.

← 2 pages

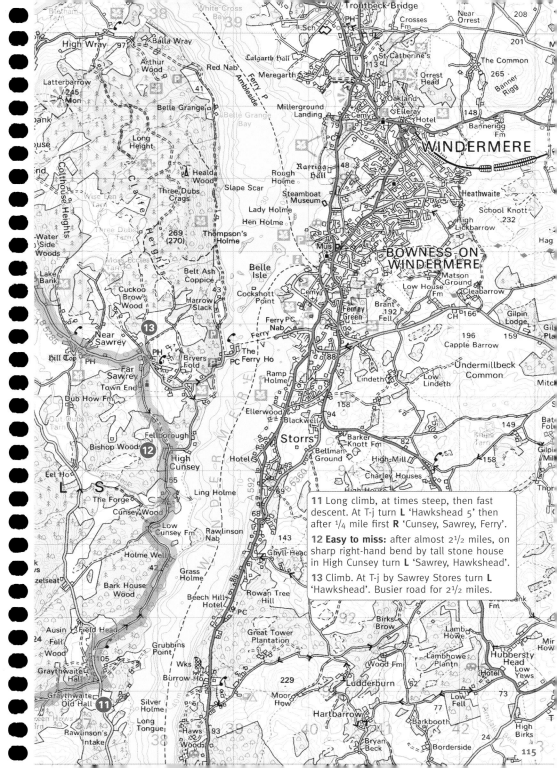

11 Long climb, at times steep, then fast descent. At T-j turn **L** 'Hawkshead 5' then after 1/4 mile first **R** 'Cunsey, Sawrey, Ferry'.

12 Easy to miss: after almost 2¹/2 miles, on sharp right-hand bend by tall stone house in High Cunsey turn **L** 'Sawrey, Hawkshead'.

13 Climb. At T-j by Sawrey Stores turn **L** 'Hawkshead'. Busier road for 2¹/2 miles.

Broughton in Furness to Coniston

Two rides start from Broughton in Furness, an attractive village in the southwest of the National Park, with several good pubs and cafés set around a fine little square. The ride leaves the village on a short section of railway path; the old railway used to link Coniston to the mainline at Foxfield. Drop down from the end of the railway path on a short rougher section to join the lanes crossing the remote and sparsely populated landscape of Woodland Fell and Subberthwaite Common, with one particularly steep climb east from Fell Gate. These

lanes are prime examples that show that it is still possible to find quiet areas in the Lake District to ride where you can avoid traffic. The River Crake, draining Coniston Water south towards Greenodd Sands and Morecambe Bay, is crossed at Lowick Bridge then you turn north on the lovely lane right alongside the eastern shore of Coniston Water, setting of *Swallows and Amazons*. Enjoy the wonderful views across the lake to the Coniston Fells. You may wish to stop at the café at Brantwood, former home of John Ruskin, to sit out on the terrace and appreciate the views. Climb then descend to Coniston, joining the network of traffic-free trails that run alongside the B5285 then along the lakeshore past the Bluebird Café and the campsites to join the A593 at Torver. The toughest climb of the day, with the first section so steep you may prefer to walk, is

on a minor road branching off the A593 and climbing to the ride's highpoint at 850ft (260m) offering panoramic views across the Furness Fells and south towards Duddon Sands and the coast. Rejoin the A593 at Lower Hawthwaite, finishing the ride with a long descent back to Broughton in Furness.

A tough challenge

One of the toughest 30-mile rides in the country starts from Broughton, following the Duddon Valley north to Ulpha, crossing Birker Fell northwest to Eskdale Green, turning east to climb Hardknott Pass, returning south down the Duddon Valley from Cockley Beck then, as a final sting in the tail, cutting south from Hall Dunnerdale up and over to Broughton Mills then back to Broughton. Try to do this midweek, outside school holidays when the roads are at their quietest.

Overview
29 miles / 47 kilometres ● Moderate

Start
Manor Arms PH, in the main square, Broughton in Furness

Parking
In square or on-street parking

Busy roads
Two sections of the A593 are used, the road can get busy at peak periods:
● Near Torver (wide, good visibility) **19** to **20**
● Near Broughton (mainly downhill) **23**

Terrain
Steep climb (410ft / 125m) up over Subberthwaite Common in the first third of the ride. Very steep climb (510ft / 155m) southwest of Torver onto Broughton Moor. The rest of the ride is fairly easy

Nearest railway
Foxfield

Refreshments
Broughton in Furness
Lots of choice

Lowick Bridge
Red Lion PH
T: 01229 885366

Brantwood
Café
T: 01539 441396

Coniston
Lots of choice

Torver
Wilson Arms PH
T: 01539 441237
Church House Inn
T: 01539 441282

Broughton Mills
(just off the route)
Blacksmiths Arms PH
T: 01229 716284

Other rides nearby

Map pages

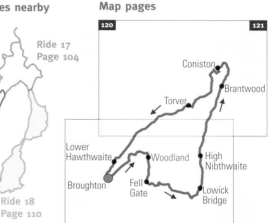

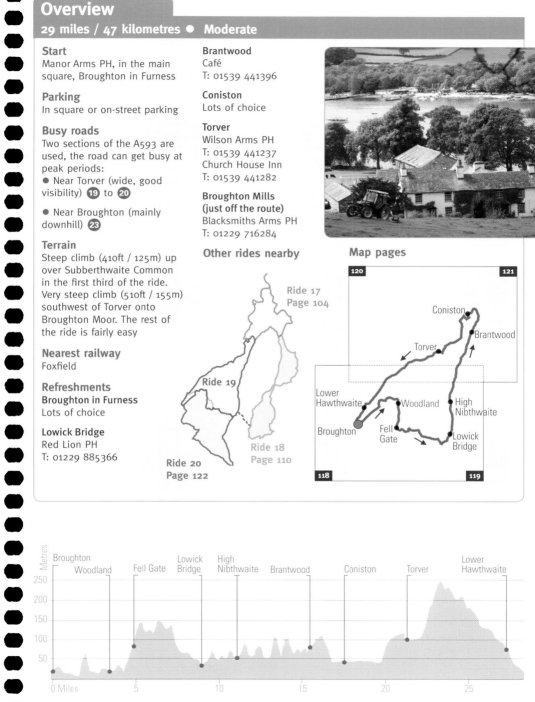

Ride 17
Page 104

Ride 19

Ride 18
Page 110

Ride 20
Page 122

120   121
Coniston
Brantwood
Torver
Lower Hawthwaite
Woodland   High Nibthwaite
Broughton   Fell Gate   Lowick Bridge
118   119

Metres
Broughton
Woodland   Fell Gate   Lowick Bridge   High Nibthwaite   Brantwood   Coniston   Torver   Lower Hawthwaite
250
200
150
100
50
0 Miles   5   10   15   20   25

22 After further 1¾ miles, at X-roads by 'Give Way' sign turn **L** gently uphill 'Broughton in Furness'.

23 At T-j after almost 2 miles turn **L** then shortly at next T-j (with A593) turn **R** 'Broughton in Furness' and follow for 1¼ miles back to start.

Ride 20 also passes through Broughton in Furness. Page 122

1 From Manor Arms PH in Broughton in Furness turn **L** downhill then shortly after garage on left, opposite right turn to Workington and Whitehaven, turn **L** through wide wooden gate onto broad stone railway path signposted 'Woodland 1½'.

2 After almost 1½ miles at end of railway path turn **R** downhill to descend on narrower, rougher track. At T-j with road turn **L**.

3 Flat section then steep climb. At T-j turn **R** on narrower lane 'Woodland'.

4 Steep descent then flat section. At T-j turn **R** 'Ulverston'.

5 Ignore two left turns. Go past church. Cross cattlegrid, ignore left turn to Ulverston, continue **SA** towards Grizebeck.

6 Start climbing steeply. At X-roads of minor lanes (your priority) just before 'Cattlegrid' road sign turn sharp **L** steeply uphill.

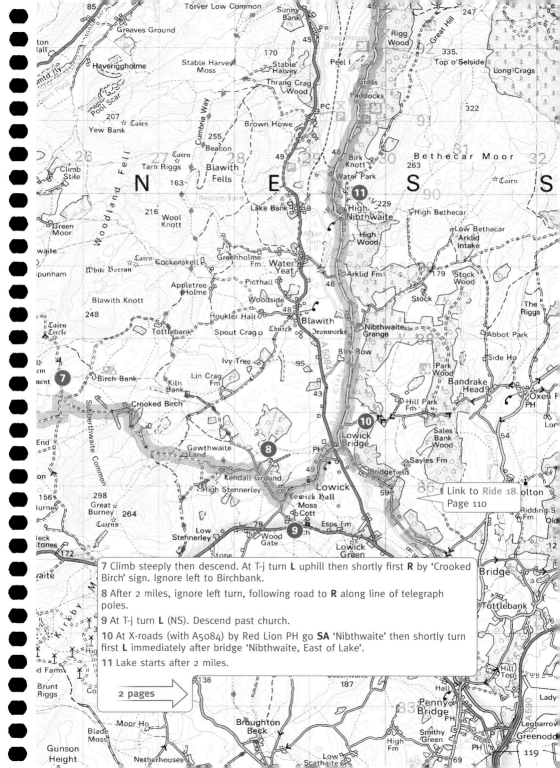

Link to **Ride 18.**
Page 110

7 Climb steeply then descend. At T-j turn **L** uphill then shortly first **R** by 'Crooked Birch' sign. Ignore left to Birchbank.

8 After 2 miles, ignore left turn, following road to **R** along line of telegraph poles.

9 At T-j turn **L** (NS). Descend past church.

10 At X-roads (with A5084) by Red Lion PH go **SA** 'Nibthwaite' then shortly turn first **L** immediately after bridge 'Nibthwaite, East of Lake'.

11 Lake starts after 2 miles.

2 pages ➡

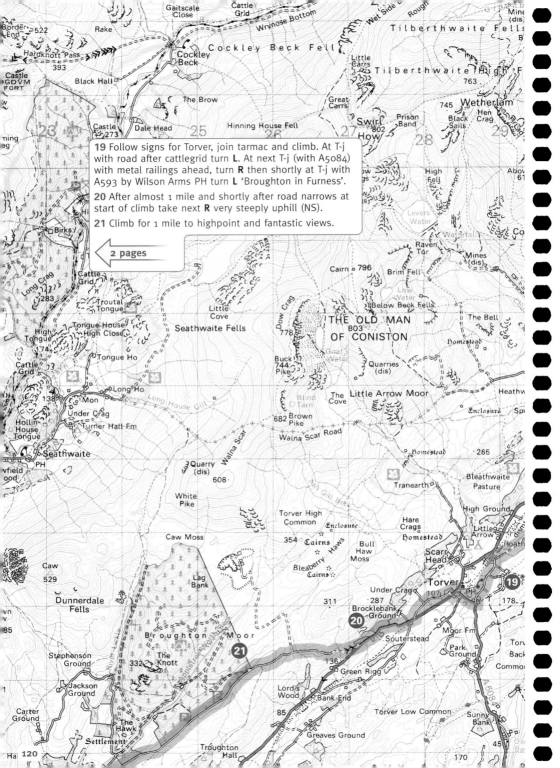

19 Follow signs for Torver, join tarmac and climb. At T-j with road after cattlegrid turn **L**. At next T-j (with A5084) with metal railings ahead, turn **R** then shortly at T-j with A593 by Wilson Arms PH turn **L** 'Broughton in Furness'.

20 After almost 1 mile and shortly after road narrows at start of climb take next **R** very steeply uphill (NS).

21 Climb for 1 mile to highpoint and fantastic views.

← 2 pages

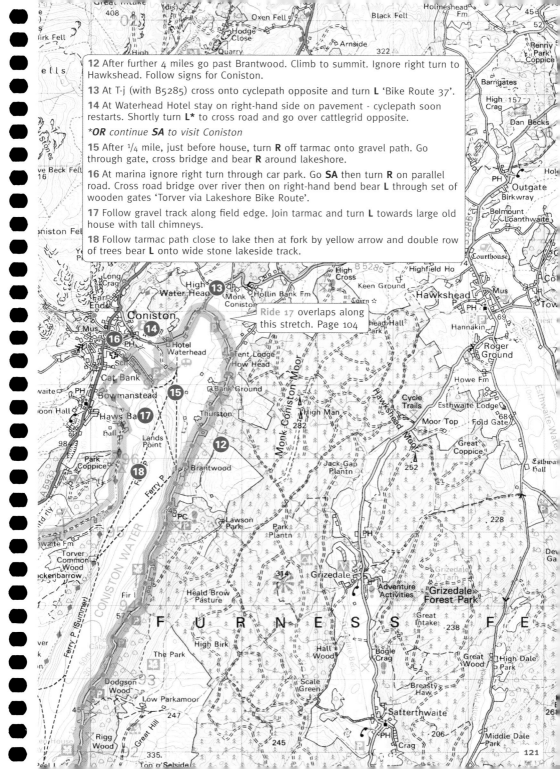

12 After further 4 miles go past Brantwood. Climb to summit. Ignore right turn to Hawkshead. Follow signs for Coniston.

13 At T-j (with B5285) cross onto cyclepath opposite and turn **L** 'Bike Route 37'.

14 At Waterhead Hotel stay on right-hand side on pavement - cyclepath soon restarts. Shortly turn **L*** to cross road and go over cattlegrid opposite.

***OR** continue **SA** to visit Coniston*

15 After ¼ mile, just before house, turn **R** off tarmac onto gravel path. Go through gate, cross bridge and bear **R** around lakeshore.

16 At marina ignore right turn through car park. Go **SA** then turn **R** on parallel road. Cross road bridge over river then on right-hand bend bear **L** through set of wooden gates 'Torver via Lakeshore Bike Route'.

17 Follow gravel track along field edge. Join tarmac and turn **L** towards large old house with tall chimneys.

18 Follow tarmac path close to lake then at fork by yellow arrow and double row of trees bear **L** onto wide stone lakeside track.

Ride 17 overlaps along this stretch. Page 104

121

Broughton to Ulverston

The final ride in the book is the second one starting from the fine little village of Broughton in Furness. Just as the other ride used a stone-based railway path at the start, so too this ride avoids the busy A595 by using two short, stone-based off-road sections, the first dropping you down at the level crossing at Foxfield, the second linking a dead-end lane to the A595 at Chapels, to the north of Kirkby-in-Furness. In between the two off-road sections is one of those pancake-flat roads that comes as a real surprise for somewhere as hilly as Cumbria. Make the most of it as the hill that follows Kirkby is one of the longest and steepest in the whole book, climbing 850ft (260m) in less than 2 miles.

If you need an excuse to stop and walk, the views that open up behind you across the Duddon Sands to Black Combe are spectacular. You deserve the long descent that follows down into Ulverston, although be aware that there are a couple of short uphills in the overall descent. The handsome market town of Ulverston is famous as the birthplace of Stan Laurel of Laurel & Hardy fame. Turn north from here on the labyrinth of lanes that criss-cross the area northeast towards the Rusland Valley. Just south of Lowick you turn northwest, climbing across the remote and little explored landscape of Subberthwaite Common and Woodland Fell. Descend then climb for a final time up to Lower Hawthwaite on the A593, setting you up for a final glide down into Broughton in Furness. If you like cakes, head for the excellent bakery!

Overview

24 miles / 39 kilometres ● Strenuous

Start
Manor Arms PH, in the main square, Broughton in Furness

Parking
In square or on-street parking

Busy roads
● The road out of Broughton can be busy **1**

● The A593 at the end of the ride is occasionally busy but the section used is mainly downhill **19** to **20**

Terrain
One very tough climb southeast from Kirkby-in-Furness (850ft / 260m). Three other noticeable climbs: from Ulverston north to Netherhouses (490ft / 150m), from Lowick west over Subberthwaite Common (360ft / 110m) and from Rosthwaite southwest to Lower Hawthwaite (295ft / 90m)

Other rides nearby

Ride 19
Page 116

Ride 20

Nearest railway
Foxfield

Refreshments
Broughton in Furness
Lots of choice

Kirkby-in-Furness
Ship PH
T: 01229 889454
Burlington Inn
T: 01229 889039

Ulverston
Lots of choice

**Lowick Bridge
(just off the route)**
Red Lion PH
T: 01229 885366

Map pages

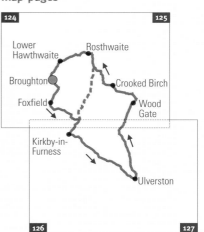

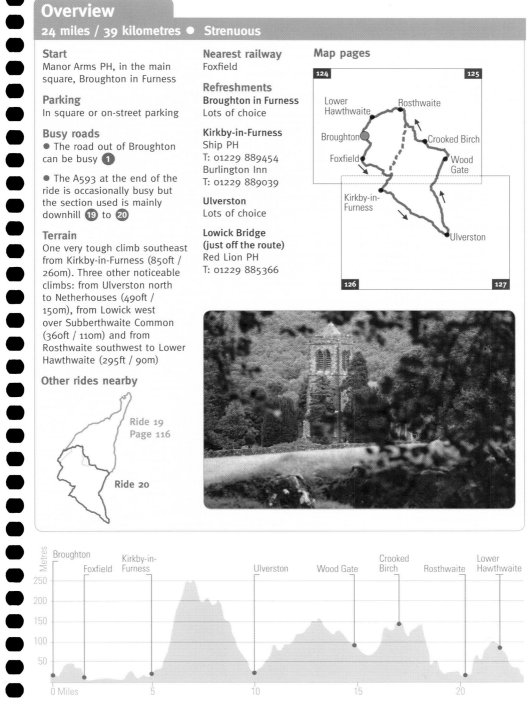

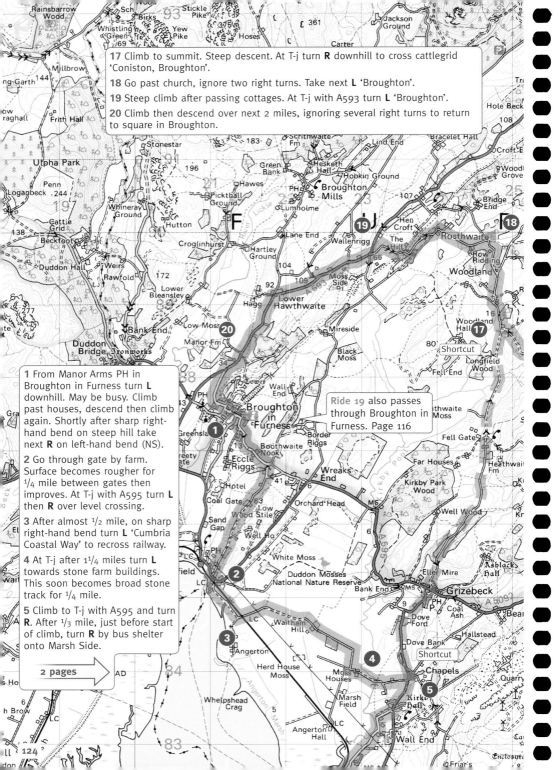

17 Climb to summit. Steep descent. At T-j turn **R** downhill to cross cattlegrid 'Coniston, Broughton'.

18 Go past church, ignore two right turns. Take next **L** 'Broughton'.

19 Steep climb after passing cottages. At T-j with A593 turn **L** 'Broughton'.

20 Climb then descend over next 2 miles, ignoring several right turns to return to square in Broughton.

Ride 19 also passes through Broughton in Furness. Page 116

1 From Manor Arms PH in Broughton in Furness turn **L** downhill. May be busy. Climb past houses, descend then climb again. Shortly after sharp right-hand bend on steep hill take next **R** on left-hand bend (NS).

2 Go through gate by farm. Surface becomes rougher for $1/4$ mile between gates then improves. At T-j with A595 turn **L** then **R** over level crossing.

3 After almost $1/2$ mile, on sharp right-hand bend turn **L** 'Cumbria Coastal Way' to recross railway.

4 At T-j after $1^1/4$ miles turn **L** towards stone farm buildings. This soon becomes broad stone track for $1/4$ mile.

5 Climb to T-j with A595 and turn **R**. After $1/3$ mile, just before start of climb, turn **R** by bus shelter onto Marsh Side.

2 pages ➡

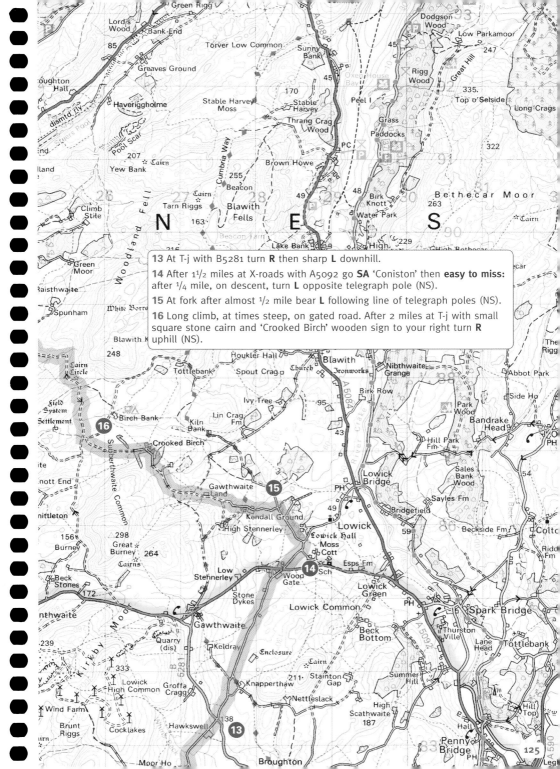

13 At T-j with B5281 turn **R** then sharp **L** downhill.

14 After 1½ miles at X-roads with A5092 go **SA** 'Coniston' then **easy to miss:** after ¼ mile, on descent, turn **L** opposite telegraph pole (NS).

15 At fork after almost ½ mile bear **L** following line of telegraph poles (NS).

16 Long climb, at times steep, on gated road. After 2 miles at T-j with small square stone cairn and 'Crooked Birch' wooden sign to your right turn **R** uphill (NS).

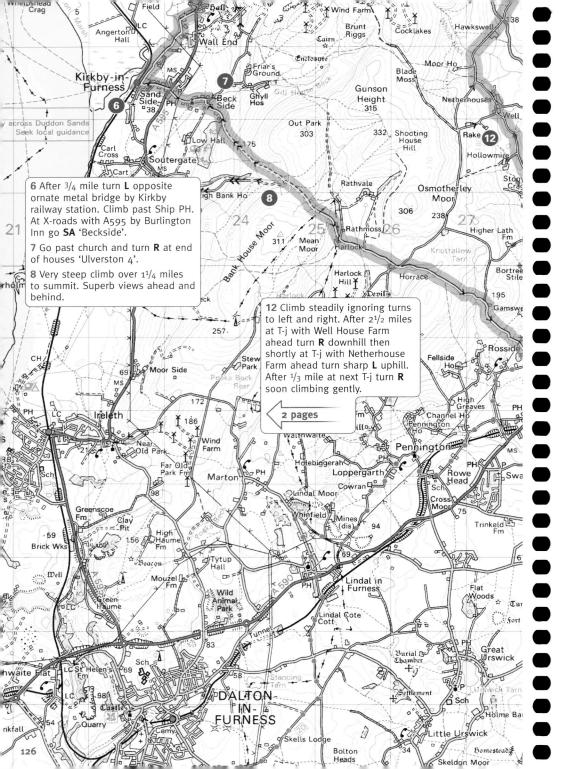

6 After 3/4 mile turn **L** opposite ornate metal bridge by Kirkby railway station. Climb past Ship PH. At X-roads with A595 by Burlington Inn go **SA** 'Beckside'.

7 Go past church and turn **R** at end of houses 'Ulverston 4'.

8 Very steep climb over 1¼ miles to summit. Superb views ahead and behind.

12 Climb steadily ignoring turns to left and right. After 2½ miles at T-j with Well House Farm ahead turn **R** downhill then shortly at T-j with Netherhouse Farm ahead turn sharp **L** uphill. After ⅓ mile at next T-j turn **R** soon climbing gently.

2 pages ←

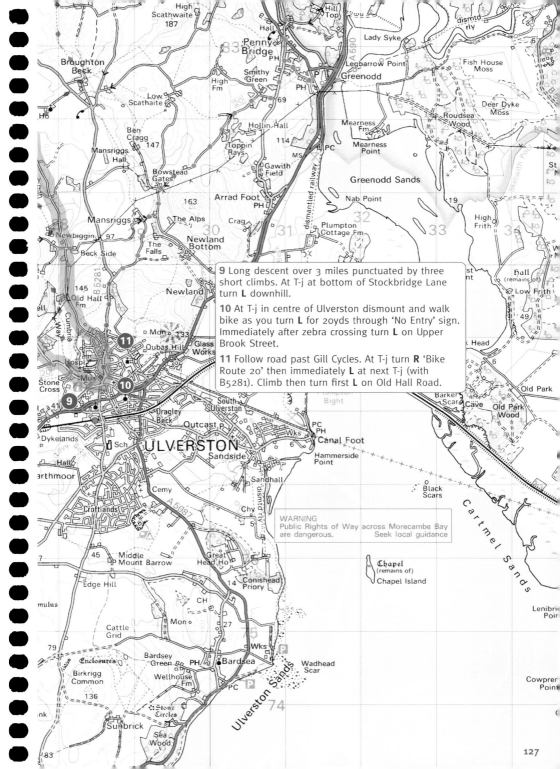

9 Long descent over 3 miles punctuated by three short climbs. At T-j at bottom of Stockbridge Lane turn **L** downhill.

10 At T-j in centre of Ulverston dismount and walk bike as you turn **L** for 20yds through 'No Entry' sign. Immediately after zebra crossing turn **L** on Upper Brook Street.

11 Follow road past Gill Cycles. At T-j turn **R** 'Bike Route 20' then immediately **L** at next T-j (with B5281). Climb then turn first **L** on Old Hall Road.

WARNING
Public Rights of Way across Morecambe Bay are dangerous.   Seek local guidance